TheShepherd purpose books series

Foreword By Dr Bitrus Audu

Purpose of Living

Live the life you
were created for

THESHEPHERD
LOHO-U-TER SHADRACH

scrollhouse

Purpose of Living
Living a fulfilled life

©2020 TheShepherd Loho-u-Ter Shadrach.
 All rights reserved.

Published by:
Scrollhouse Publishing Firm.
A Service of TheShepherd Loho-u-Ter Resources
Zaria Road, Mission Street
Farin Gada, Jos.
Plateau State

No part of this book may be reproduced in any written, electronic, recording, or photocopying form without written permission of the author and publishers.

ISBN: 978-978-54440-1-8

For special discounts for bulk purchases, please contact:
08053468634 | 08032988168
Scrollhouseng@gmail.com
Visit www.scrollhouse.com.ng for eBooks

Layout and Cover Design: TheShepherd Loho-u-Ter Shadrach

Printed Nigeria by Triune Concept

Dedication

To the Creator of life who puts in every person the purpose of living.

Acknowledgments

I give thanks to the Creator of heaven and earth, the preserver of life, the giver of wisdom and insight, who plants the purpose of every person in them.

I appreciate my wife Salome, and my children Shalman and Sharon Loho-u-Ter and Godwin Knpamor for having confidence in me for this project. This encourages me to do more.

I acknowledge people who have sat under my teachings and practically contributed or asked questions to make me study some more.

My thanks go to my editors—Emeka Opara, Lydia Torkwase Chile, Iliya Mangvwat and Muyamba Mathias, and the team at Scrollhouse Publishing Company for making sure that this work meets international standards.

My special thanks go to my readers. I appreciate the confidence you have in me, and in my ability to influence your lives.

Foreword

Everyone has a God-designed purpose that must be discerned and discovered or else life would not make sense. Knowing the creator's purpose for one's life, is therefore, the greatest knowledge of life. Fulfilling His purpose for one's life, on the other hand, is the greatest life accomplishment. The value of one's life in the after-life hinges on this truth.

Several years ago I taught a series on the topic of purpose. The responses from people made me realize that more of such teachings need to be heard. Unfortunately, such vital teachings on purpose are not as pronounced these days as they should be. Thus many people live their lives without a specific direction.

I was excited therefore, when the author met me after a meeting, asking that I write a foreword for his book, "Purpose of living." This reconnected me to the teachings I had done. My first response, however, was to tell him I would not have the time to write. I had a pile of things to attend to, ranging from travels to speaking engagements and supervision of some doctoral dissertations. I nonetheless, asked that the manuscript be mailed to me. On glancing at the table of content and quickly gleaning through the script, I knew that this was not those types of books one pushes aside. From my observation of and interaction with the author, I know he is not only a man who has a clear purpose but one who is living it out. I believe he is worth reading or listening to on the subject.

In the book, TheShepherd Loho-u-Ter Shadrach used the most basic English for most readers, including children from the later part of primary school to read and understand. For me, his simple style of writing makes the book really unique. This then implies that, knowing one's purpose must be given attention from an early age in life. The earlier a person knows their purpose, the easier to fulfill it.

The author states that all people are created for God's glory, for relationships and for service, but then he said that everyone has a personal purpose that is unique to them. This is where he really caught my attention. While there are several books on purpose, many authors fail to elaborate on people's unique purposes. To be fulfilled in life, a person's personal purpose must be pursued along with the general purpose. Failure to do so may lead many to live a life without focus.

The height of this book is the diagnostic test that helps people discover their individual purposes and its illustrations. The vivid illustrations are the type that keeps readers seated at the edge of their chairs and glued to the book till they munch all the content to the end. I got to understand that there are other books on the purpose series that Shadrach has written. In light of all the above, I strongly recommend this book and indeed all the others on the series without hesitation.

Dr. Bitrus Audu

Content

1.Introduction

Efforts and encouragement are not
 enough without purpose and direction.
-John F. Kennedy

I THOUGHT THAT I KNEW IT ALL AND NEEDED no help to discover my life purpose. I just kept trying one thing or the other. I would move on when one thing did not go well. Little did I know that I was wasting precious time. Now that I have discovered what I was created for, life seems to be more interesting. My life now does not consist of the things I have but in what I think my Maker wants me to do.

Created to enjoy

I must say that one of the most challenging things about life is ignorance about the purpose a person was created for. Discovering your life purpose is very crucial to living and enjoying life. Surely, you were not created to endure this life but enjoy it, so it is necessary to discover your purpose for living to fully enjoy life. This is very key to unlocking all that your creator meant for you to enjoy.

If someone was to ask you your life purpose, what will be your answer? As simple as this question may seem, the answer is not that simple. In fact, you may have been struggling to answer the question the moment I asked. Maybe because you have done a lot of things in your life that you seemed to think were your life purpose. A closer look at your life, however, informs you that life is rather a constant pain.

Nothing was in vain

Sometimes people think that if they are doing a nice job, then, they are living a purposeful life. Yes, it is true that everything you have done with your life was not in vain, and I mean even the stupid things. The several stages you have passed through in life definitely have something to contribute in shaping your destiny. Your dissatisfaction with many of the things you have done informed you that you were in the wrong place. This may have pushed you further to the search in the bid to discover what you were created for.

There is a whole big world out there filled with life coaches. Some of the coaches will not help you discover what you were created for but will introduce you to a mirage. This makes them a rallying point that forces you to keep coming back to them to ask questions about life and direction on how to live. I am not that kind of coach, which is why I am writing this material to help you discover the general and personal purpose for living. This makes you know the direction of life and helps you enjoy life to the maximum.

You can discover your purpose

There are actually three main purposes for which you were created and I call them *Tripartite Life Purposes*. There is however a personal purpose you must discover to be able to properly tap in to maximize the worth of the tripartite life purposes. The truth of the matter is, no matter how much I want you to know your personal life purpose, only you can discover it. In this book *"Purpose of Living"*, I will take time to explain the purposes the creator designated to every human, and I believe that the knowledge will help you to put more value on life and further help you to discover your life purpose.

Do not think that if you have an understanding of your life purpose, this book is not for you. You will be surprised that after reading this book, you will hold firm to your purpose. This book is also a refresher material for those that go through challenges of this life and are confused on what the creator will have them do. I plead with you that whatever it takes, make sure you read this book to the end. I am a hundred percent sure that your enemy does not want you to read this book because he knows that your life will improve tremendously. Keep going, you can rest at some point to do other stuff, but never give up on this book until you have finished reading it. Now let's go!

2.Purpose Retardants

The envious die not once, but as
oft as the envied win applause.
-**Baltasar Gracian**

THERE ARE MANY PEOPLE WHO SEEM TO know what they were created for. The challenge, however, is that they are yet to properly get a firm grip on what they think they are supposed to do for life. I had reasons to discourse with Sade Akanni, a great woman of high repute many years ago, she told me that the Creator relates to us on some matters about our lives for our information, meaning that you may know what you want to do with your life but the road to get there will not always be smooth.

It is commonly said, "Rome was not built in a day." There is no magic wand, prayer or session with a life coach that will automatically land you into your destiny. In most cases, you know your life purpose but getting there takes a lot of work and determination. To survive purpose retardants who try to make sure you do not achieve your goal, you must stay focused.

I will try to mention a few of these retardants. The list is not, however, exhausted, you can discover the others for yourself.

The purpose retardants include:

Self

One of the greatest threats to your destiny is you. Unfortunately, people always point accusing fingers to others as to why they are not succeeding in life. They fail to understand that one's inability to discover his or her destiny can actually be the biggest hindrance to success.

I have noticed that several people have the wrong definition of a successful life in the first place. They think their purpose for living is to primarily make money and accumulate wealth, for this reason, they think their lives are over when they do not see money coming in as they expect it to come. Friend! Life is more than just accumulating wealth. It is more of doing what you were created for.

You are your greatest asset

You are your greatest asset. What you see, hear, eat, think, and touch can go a long way to mar or make you. If you really want to move forward, you need to stop injecting negativity into your life by the things that you may have contact with. You must give attention especially when the things you relate with; affect the way you think.

You can be the retardant to your destiny. This is done by being careless with discovering your purpose for living and blaming others for the way your life is. You have all it takes to succeed. You were created by default for a reason and your creator put all you were meant to be in you. People who are conversant with the *life-manual[1]* tend to discover and live in synchronization to their purpose better.

Health

No matter the worth deposited in you, an unhealthy body will retard what you were created for. Living

___

[1] I have used the term Life-manual or the manufacturer's manual for the Holy Bible is this book extensively.

healthy is not all about having a great body, it goes beyond that to having a healthy mind. No matter how clear you see your personal life purpose, an unhealthy body will slow you down and if there is further neglect, your life will be cut short and your purpose for living will be thwarted.

What you eat is very key to having a healthy life. To enjoy a healthy life, you must strive to eat a balanced diet. A balanced diet gives your body the nutrition it needs to function properly. Getting the majority of your daily calories from fresh fruits and vegetables, whole grains, and lean proteins is the best way of getting calories your body deserves.

Eat balanced foods that are high in vitamins, minerals, and other nutrients and low in unnecessary fats and sugars. The following are essential parts of a balanced diet:

Fruits: They are a great source of nutrition than quick and tasty snacks.

Vegetables: They are the primary source of essential vitamins and minerals. Dark, leafy greens generally contain the most nutrition and you should try to eat them at every meal.

Grains: Whole grains that are prepared using the entire grain, including the hull, provide more nutrition. Do not be carried away by class and the good look of processed grains. The best part of the grain is gone with the hull if you process it.

Proteins: Meats, nuts, and beans are primary sources of protein. These are essential for proper muscle and brain development. Avoid the fatty parts of meat to reduce the amount of fat and cholesterol intake in your body.

Dairy: Dairy products provide calcium, vitamin D, and other essential nutrients. They are however, also a major source of fat. It is, therefore, best to choose reduced-fat or fat-free cheeses, milk, and yoghurt.

Oils: Oils should be used sparingly. Opt for low-fat versions of products that contain oil, such as salad dressing and mayonnaise. Good oils, such as olive oil, can replace fattier vegetable oil in your diet. Avoid foods that have been deep-fried in oil because they contain a large number of empty calories. [2]

---

[2] Healthline, "Achieving a Balanced Diet," [cited July 27, 2015] Online: https://www.healthline.com/health/balanced-diet#AchievingaBalancedDiet4.

The importance of having a balanced diet cannot be overemphasized. Many people who would have lived longer to impact their generations were cut short due to the negligence of their bodies by their eating habits.

You also need exercise and rest

Apart from eating a balanced diet, exercise and proper rest are essentials to a healthy body. If you do not give attention to your body, it will slow you down and retard your purpose for living. Do not take this point for granted, and never think handling your body carelessly is limited to eating much. Sometimes religion pushes people to think the body needs to be neglected for their inner self to prosper. For your life to take proper shape, both your outer and your inner being needs the attention necessary for proper functionality. No wonder the life manual says:

> For physical training is of some value (useful for a little), but godliness (spiritual training) is useful *and* of value in everything *and* in every way, for it holds promise for the present life and also for the life which is to come. [3]

---

[3] 1 Timothy 4:8. Amplified Bible.

People

Sometimes I do not understand why other people think they know what is best for you. They condemn everything you do and suggest all manner of things they feel they are good for you without finding out if you would like what they are suggesting.

I know parents want what is best for their children. Unfortunately, some parents push their children beyond the boundaries. I will not be surprised that at a grown-up age of over thirty, some parents may still be detecting to their children what they should be doing. Now do not misunderstand me. There is nothing wrong with parents advising their children, but there is everything wrong for parents to think that whatever advice they give their children; they must work with it.

Beware of wrong counsel

If you do not take time, friends and family will retard your purpose in life. They will give you wrong advice purposefully, and after ten years you will discover that you deviated from what you were created for.

I have done a lot of jobs in my life, some I did to keep busy while others I enjoyed for a while. I had to let go of some because I discovered they were not the primary reason I was created for. I was at a time working with an organization, I did a lot of exploits (so I was told), but discovered that the organization served just as a foundation to get me to where I was going. I made up my mind and resigned after serving the organization for ten years. And I tell you, people started convincing me out of love that, the best place for me was to get back to the organization.

Beware of side attractions

When you are on a journey into destiny, there will be several side attractions that may seem to look good at the time. Never look at those distractions that will sway you away from your vision. If you do, you will end up discovering that you wasted unnecessary time. Do not allow people to retard you from your aim in life, even if you seem to be delayed, hold firm to your purpose and what you are persuaded God is telling you to do and you will laugh at last.

Job

So you think you cannot survive without your present job? How were you living before you got there? For some of you, your job is actually what is delaying you from having a firm grip on your destiny. You are afraid of how life will be without the job. Fortunately, you have full knowledge as to what your purpose for living is, unfortunately, you are holding tight to your job and you know full well that your time to leave that job is long overdue.

God could be leading otherwise

Do you know that your breakthrough will never come in your present job no matter how much money you are making? This is especially for those who clearly know that God is leading them otherwise. Do not misunderstand breakthroughs to financial wealth. Financial wealth without the satisfaction in what you are doing amounts to failure and disgrace to your destiny. No matter how good your current job seems to be, if the inner satisfaction is not there, you would have wasted your time.

Money is not everything

I have seen the most frustrated people have so much money. I am aware that many financially wealthy people are on drugs and are involved with terrible vices to cover up for their inner void to no avail. If you think that money is everything, then you know nothing. The rich also cry.

I strongly believe that money is your slave and it has no right to control you except you allow it. Staying on a job because you afraid to lose money will hinder you from making giant strides in life which will lead you to that life you will enjoy despite all odds. More so, you may be surprised that if you stay where you are persuaded to stay, money will begin to serve you at your beckoning.

Time and Location

The life manual records the saying of the wisest man that ever lived in ancient times to have said:

> I have observed something else under the sun. The fastest runner doesn't always win the race, and the strongest warrior doesn't always win the battle. The wise sometimes go hungry, and the skilful are not necessarily wealthy. And those who are educated don't always lead successful lives. It is all decided by chance, by being in the right place at the right time.[4]

---

[4] Ecclesiastes 9:11. New Living Translation.

It is generally believed that when you run fast you win a race. There are, however, rules to winning races. You could reach the end of the line but if the race requires that you stay on your lane but you strayed, you would have lost the race. In such a race, running fast is inconsequential since running on track is the requirement.

Life essentials are not everything

Skills, strength, wisdom, and education are very essential to living a successful life. Others have employed all of these but their lives seem to be a merry-go-round. With all they have done, they cannot put a finger on their life purpose.

If your life purpose is to reach out to patients in war-torn countries as a surgeon, you have no business staying in Abuja, Lagos, or New York where there is no war going on. If you were to influence your nation politically, you have no business working in the bank. As long as you stay in the wrong place, you cannot fulfill your life purpose.

Right timing

You could as well be in the right location, but your creator may tell you not to make any move just yet.

He may just be asking you to observe. Rushing into what you think is your life purpose at the wrong time will amount to frustration. Some missed their timing and the enemy suggested they were not in the right location and they derailed.

Waiting is a virtue that needs to be imbibed. The key to your life purpose is *being in the right place at the right time* even if you seem to know your life purpose.

My candid advice to you is that you check your life and where you stay. It may be time for you to move. It could be that you were in the right location but your time there is up. Do not waste any more time, get moving as you hold fast on your purpose for living in your next location where your allocation will locate you.

Insecurity

The challenge of insecurity is almost becoming a global occurrence, and everyone must learn to cope with insecurity. There are sometimes, simple security awareness and self-defence techniques that are capable of preserving one's life. There are other situations that insecurity becomes unbearable, as all activities to normal life; work, schools, and buying and selling are at a halt because of war.

If you are in a war-torn zone, sometimes getting to live your purpose may be difficult. Except if war forms part of your life purpose. This does not, however, mean that because there is war, a person should fold his or her arms and do nothing. You may be surprised that in the midst of insurgency, your eyes will be opened to what you will be doing in the meanwhile.

Never give up on your life purpose because of the insecurities around you. Try to find a way around them and see how you can take advantage of the insurgencies to spring forth into your purpose and live the life you were created to live.

Religion

There are some people that, staying around them is really a pain in the neck. They will hardly say anything without mentioning God or Allah. The annoying part is that their lives are not commensurate with the so much talk about their God. Such people attribute even their laziness to God. Instead of going out to look for a job by actually applying for one, they are there trusting God. Instead of telling a girl I love you and I want to marry you, they are trusting God. Instead of going to school they tell you that God does not want them to school but serve him. It is true that a god can say that to people depending on which god it is. The challenge is that the lives of such people do not show in any way that their lives are in line with purposeful living.

What kind of god is that?

It is true that one of the general purposes of living is to serve God. But when a person's life is almost useless to himself or herself, family, community, and the state, it is questionable which god such a person is really serving. God's intention is not to make people earthly useless in the name of religion.

What God tells his followers to tie a bomb around their bodies, detonating it to kill both themselves and others? What god thwarts other people from fulfilling their destinies in the name of God? Religion is a cancer and for you to serve God properly you must cut it away from your life and have a real relationship with God.

Purpose is not religious fanatism

The question I ask some of these religious fanatics is if they have a brain at all. They say the Lord says in every sentence as if they were some robots that do not have a brain of their own. Do not misunderstand me to mean living a sincere life is religious fanatism. When I talk about religious fanatism, I mean a religious life that fails to relate with fellow humans who may not understand a person's religious view. Such are the people that disrespect and dehumanize others in the name of religion. They think every other person is a sinner except the people in their group.

I believe that if you properly relate with your creator the way you should, religion will not form part of your purpose retardants. We need God and not a religion if you ask me.

3.Purpose Reinventing

We must reinvent a future
free of blinders so that we
can choose from real options.
-David Suzuki

TO REINVENT MEANS TO CREATE AGAIN something that was once created. Every manufacturer has in mind what they want in their invention. Failure for an invention to accomplish the manufacturer's desire is the failure of such a product. Most inventors recycle products that do not meet the manufacturer's specifications. The inability to recognize that you were meant for a purpose will actually hinder you from realizing your life purpose.

You were born for a purpose

Paul the apostle said, *"I don't care about my own life. The most important thing is that I complete my mission..."*[5] Your manufacturer made you for a purpose and you are special in His sight. King David of ancient times knew this fact and said, *"I praise you because you made me in an amazing and wonderful way, what you have done is wonderful. I know this very well."*[6]

Your greatest undoing is to let anyone (and that includes you), look down on you and make you feel useless and un-purposeful. Your life is very important to your manufacturer even if you are not proud of your background. Rick Warren confirms this saying, "Many Children are unplanned by their parents, but they are not unplanned by God. God's purpose took into account human error and even sin."[7] Your background does not matter to God. He has great plans for you no matter who you are. Even if you consider your background to be discouraging, the life manual affirms your importance with the words of God saying, *"I am your Creator. You were*

---

5 Acts 20:24 New Century Version.
6 Psalm 139:14. New Century Version.
7 Rick Warren. *Purpose Driven Life*, (Grand Rapids: Zondervan, 2002), 23.

in my care even before you were born..."[8] Wow! this kind of love is huge.

Ignorance births abuse

When people do not understand their purpose in life, abuse is inevitable. Abuse to themselves and others. I have seen people kill themselves bit by bit from careless living. I have had encounters with people who are gradually killing themselves from drunkenness, illicit drugs, smoking, sexual immorality, and several other dangerous vices.

The enemy's agenda is to steal, kill and to destroy you. He may have corrupted your life like what a virus does to a computer. For you to make headway, you must go to the manufacturer's default. The co-manufacturer had to make sure that you have all that it takes to operate optimally and this is what he said, "The thief comes only in order to steal and kill and destroy. I came that they may have *and* enjoy life, and have it in abundance (to the full, till it overflows)."[9]

---

[8] Isaiah 44:2. Contemporary English Version.
[9] John 10:10. Amplified Bible.

Default mode

The importance of your purpose for living will require you to get hold of the manufacturer's manual and discover how you were originally meant to operate. It could also mean you are actually operating according to the manufacturer's manual but you missed out on your personal purpose for living. You got it right. You were doing so well until family and friends convinced you that you were not making enough money. If you just held on a little longer, you would have had so much by now but you opted out.

There are times you think you should go back to your original purpose but you feel you have left that part of your life for too long and so you are concerned about what people will think of you. It is better to reinvent your purpose and get the whole bliss of life rather than staying where you are and suffer in silence.
People may say you are a great person but deep within you; something is missing until you go back to your default mode.

I will take time in the next chapters to relate the general purposes the manufacturer has created all humans for. This does not, however, mean you cannot add other applications in your life to make your life better. Any life application is welcome if such applications are not divergent to the Creator's manual.

4. Purpose for Living

The only failure one should
fear is not hugging to the
purpose they see as best.
-**George Eliot**

THE HYPE OF SUCCESS HAS LED MANY people to believe that living a successful life is living a materially wealthy life and having power. This quest has made people go extra miles regardless of the means to get money and power. This they soon discover there is still a big vacuum in their lives that is yet to be filled. Others have resorted to all manner of spiritual pursuits outside the manufacturer's manual, but also discovered that the void actually expanded.

It is not all about ourselves

I wanted to know other people's understanding of the discourse of purpose and it landed me in some discoveries. Dorothy Firman, Ed.D., is a psychotherapist and author/editor of many books including *Chicken Soup for the Mother and Daughter Soul*. She has also authored "Living a Life of Purpose." This is what she said about the purpose of living:

> **Living a Life of Purpose** is about asking the biggest question, WHY and the most pressing question, HOW. This is about hearing the Call of Self and answering, in every way that we can. This is all we have, our own truth, our own choices. No matter the ups and downs, and there will be plenty, we live in a constant state of possibility, opening more and more to our own lived purpose.[10]

Firman's explanation for a life of purpose is very catchy. What I do not understand with what Firman says is that she never made mention of what is the

---

[10] Psychology Today, "Living life purpose," [cited July 27, 2015] Online:
https://www.psychologytoday.com/blog/living-life-purpose.

manufacturer's intent for creating people is. She said purpose is about, "hearing the Call of Self and answering, in every way that we can. This is all we have, our own truth, our own choices." This explanation reminds me of some of the Hollywood movies where a robot begins to operate independently of the manufacturer, becoming a god in themselves. This trend, unfortunately, is becoming popular where the issues of a person's purpose are discussed. Many people think it is all about themselves and there is nothing to do with their maker.

God must be involved

Frank Sonnenberg agrees that everyone has their individual purposes but outlines seven general threads that bind a life with purpose. The seven points include:

   i. Live by your beliefs and values:
  ii. Set priorities.
 iii. Follow your passion.
  iv. Achieve balance.
   v. Feel content:
  vi. Make a difference

vii.   Live in the moment"[11]

The points Frank raised are very vital, yet he also did not lay emphasis on where the creator of human beings comes in. Unfortunately, people are more at home if you tell them how powerful they can become without some hand of a divine being.

Stories abound of movie stars, musicians, top politicians and an array of people who seemed to have got everything right in life yet committed suicide. Most of these people had their personal life coaches who seem to have guided them to the achievements they got. A life coach who does not point to you that you have a specific manufacturer make of you is not telling you the whole truth.

This cannot be it

My tribal people say, to live is to eat food with meat. This makes people from my tribe to pay so much attention to meat as if life consists in the abundance of meat you eat. I have heard people say, they live to have sex, drink alcohol and make money. What kind

---

[11] Frank Sonnenberg. "7 ways to live life with a purpose," [cited July 27, 2015] Online: https://www.franksonnenbergonline.com/blog/7-ways-to-live-life-with-a-purpose/.

of life is that? True to it, I have seen people live this kind of life into their old age just to discover that their life was a total waste.

Writing from a new dimension

So many people have undertaken to write books on purpose, I would have let this slide but our creator communicates to us differently even when he is saying the same thing. He uses others to explain things to people of a specific region or group. Because of the magnitude and the importance of our life purpose, I will give attention to explaining purpose in the simplest way.

In the next three chapters, I'll focus on the three major purposes for which you were created, hoping that these tripartite purposes will help to shape your life and put you on the proper pedestal to your destiny.

5. Purpose for Living: Created for Gods Glory

God cannot use you as He
wishes until you come into
the fullness of His Glory.
-George Washington Carver

GOD EXPRESSLY SAYS IN THE LIFE MANUAL, "I want them back, every last one who bears my name, every man, woman, and child whom I created for my glory, yes, personally formed and made each one."[12] He created you for His own glory.

For by him, all things were created, in heaven and on earth, visible and invisible, whether thrones or

---

[12] Isaiah 43:7. The Message.

dominions or rulers or authorities—all things were created through him and for him.[13]

This is so soothing to hear that the creator of heaven and earth would say this of humans.

You have a choice

Your life is not about you but about him. He, however, does not keep a club over your head detecting how you should glorify him. This makes me wonder how people will write volumes of books about your life purpose without directing you to discover how the creator actually wants this life to be lived. Living your daily life should be to glorify God. I will, however, point out some ways you can glorify your creator.

Created for worship

The wise king Solomon was giving some wisdom tips and when he came to the conclusion of his talk he said.

All has been heard; the end of the matter is: Fear God [revere and worship Him, knowing that He is] and keep His commandments, for this is the

---

[13] Colossians 1:16. English Standard Version.

whole of man [the full, original purpose of his creation, the object of God's providence, the root of character, the foundation of all happiness, the adjustment to all inharmonious circumstances and conditions under the sun] and the whole [duty] for every man.[14]

Wow! Solomon captured this so well. Your responsibility as a person is to obey God. The easiest way to understand him is to read the manufacturers manual which is his Word—The Bible. Worshiping him is your duty. In fact, the creator says, "The people I made especially for myself, a people custom-made to praise me."[15] Worshiping him is not limited by forms but a daily life of obedience is required to keep on track.

Do not be cheated out of worship

I have gone to some meetings where I was overwhelmed by his presence and poured out my heart to worship. I have, however, gone to some places where worshipping him with all expressions is understood as showmanship. Do not allow anyone to cheat you out of what you were created to do—to worship God

---

[14] Ecclesiastes 12:13. Amplified Bible.
[15] Isaiah 43:21. The Message.

Created for dominion

After the Creator-God made an end to every other creation. He left the best for the last. The life manual says of the creation of human beings as follows:

> Let Us [Father, Son, and Holy Spirit] make mankind in Our image, after Our likeness, and let them have complete authority over the fish of the sea, the birds of the air, the [tame] beasts, and over all of the earth, and over everything that creeps upon the earth.[16]

Having dominion and authority over the earth is very key to your existence. You cannot afford to let the earth and all other creatures call the shots as to how you should live. You are in charge. You are the leader. You are the boss. Your leadership role and your ability to care for all other creatures God has made show how much you glorify him.

Created for reproduction

After God created the first man, he noticed his loneliness and quickly said, "It isn't good for the man to live alone. I need to make a suitable partner for

---

[16] Genesis 1:26. Amplified Bible.

him..."[17] This he went ahead to take action and this is what he did:

> So the LORD God made him [man] fall into a deep sleep, and he took out one of the man's ribs. Then after closing the man's side, the LORD made a woman out of the rib. The LORD God brought her to the man, and the man exclaimed, "Here is someone like me! She is part of my body, my own flesh, and bones. She came from me, a man. So I will name her Woman!"[18]

God clearly made man and woman as the means by which reproduction would take place. He made Adam and Eve, not Adam and Steve. He "created humans to be like himself; he made men and women. God gave them his blessing and said: Have a lot of children! Fill the earth with people and bring it under your control."[19] Giving birth to children is another way of glorifying the creator of the whole universe.

---

[17] Genesis 2:18. Contemporary English Version.
[18] Genesis 2: 21-23. Contemporary English Version.
[19] Genesis 1:27-28. Contemporary English Version.

Feelings may be deceptive

The world system is turning things upside down to glorify self. The reproduction means by default is being abused. Men now marry men and women marry women. The world system now says, "If it feels right, then it is right." I will not mince words to say that no matter how it feels good to have sex with a man if you are a man it is bad, and women having sex with women is also bad. The life manual says of such people:

> They claim to be wise, but they are fools. They don't worship the glorious and eternal God... So God let these people go their own way. They did what they wanted to do, and their filthy thoughts made them do shameful things with their bodies. They gave up the truth about God for a lie, and they worshiped God's creation instead of God, who will be praised forever. Amen. God let them follow their own evil desires. Women no longer wanted to have sex in a natural way, and they did things with each other that were not natural. Men behaved in the same way. They stopped wanting to have sex with women and had strong desires for sex with other men. They did shameful things

with each other, and what has happened to them is punishment for their foolish deeds.[20]

What baffles me is that same-sex married partners want to adopt children who come from man and woman. This kind of aberration is not part of the creator's way of raising children and must be rejected by people who are willing to live the life they were created to live.

Created for access

There are times I like to live in the quietness of a particular confinement, but I hate loneliness. Your creator made you to have access to him at all times. Mike Harland and Stan Moser say,

> He deeply desires a personal relationship with each one of us, and He is at work around us at all times. Just as God walked and talked with Adam and Eve in the Garden of Eden, so He desires to fellowship and communicate with each of us.[21]

---

[20] Romans 1:22-24. Contemporary English Version.
[21] Mike Harland and Stan Moser, *Seven Words of worship: the key to a lifetime of experiencing God,* (Nashville, Tennessee: B&H Publishing Group, 2008), 11.

Access denied

I can imagine him coming to the garden to relate with our first parents (Adam and Eve) on a daily basis, yet one day they disobeyed him and were afraid to come before him. Scripture says of their disobedience as follows:

> When they heard the sound of him [GOD] strolling in the garden in the evening breeze, the Man and his Wife hid in the trees of the garden, hid from GOD. GOD called to the Man: "Where are you?"[22]

This was the beginning of a severed relationship between humans and the creator. This disobedience made Him punish the man and his wife and the tempter who caused this wonderful couples to disobey their creator. Several years passed and he sent one of the core creators to fix the issues relating to our access to him which is sin. These words came up in the reunion process:

---

[22] Genesis 3:8-9. The Message.

Access granted

THEREFORE, SINCE we are justified (acquitted, declared righteous, and given a right standing with God) through faith, let us [grasp the fact that we] have [the peace of reconciliation to hold and to enjoy] peace with God through our Lord Jesus Christ (the Messiah, the Anointed One).

Through Him also we have [our] **access** (**entrance, introduction**) by faith into this grace (state of God's favour) in which we [firmly and safely] stand. And let us rejoice and exult in our hope of experiencing and enjoying the glory of God. [23]

Whereas the tempter cut you short from gaining access to your creator, the co-creator sacrificed himself and this is what the life manual says:

For he is our peace, who made both one, and brake down the middle wall of partition, having abolished in the flesh the enmity, (even) the law of commandments (contained) in ordinances; that he might create in himself of the two one new man, (so) making peace; and might

---

[23] Romans 5:1-2. Amplified Bible.

reconcile them both in one body unto God through the cross, having slain the enmity thereby: and he came and preached peace to you that were far off, and peace to them that were nigh: for through him we both have our access in one Spirit unto the Father.[24]

Since you are now reconciled with him (if you really are), you must at all times glorify him as you connect your inner person to him, be it in congregational prayer meetings or your private prayer time. For his Word says, "Be unceasing in prayer [praying perseveringly]."[25]

Created for reverence

In talking about reverence here, I am not referring to worship, even though you could use the words to mean the same. In this context, I will be referring to reverence as a sincere lifestyle.

There are several times that people try to call the shots on how you should live your life. They tell you everybody is doing it. I want to emphatically tell you that not everybody is doing it.

---

[24] Ephesians 2:14-18. American Standard Version.
[25] 1 Thessalonians 5:17. Amplified Bible.

Do you know when you tell people you are not in the habit of flirting with other women, people seem to think you are out of your mind? Sometimes when it comes to extramarital relationships and you tell the tempter you are married, the answer in many cases is, "and so what? I am also married. Everybody is doing it."

You are absurd

I have watched movies where peer groups laugh people to scorn when they discover they are virgins. Now, the only way to really know if a boy is a virgin is if he says he is, but when it comes to most women, the hymen is there as a protective door to protect their virginity. You should not think of your virginity to be absurd if you are still a virgin. In fact, you should be proud of it if you are one.

God created you to glorify him with your life. Living a decent life is a life of reverence to him. The pressures around you may suggest you live carelessly to make ends meet and probably fit in. Do not ever think you were made to fit in because you were not. You are rather meant to stand out and glorify your creator by living a holy life. He verily says, "As obedient children, do not conform to the evil desires you had when you lived in ignorance. But just as he who called you is holy, so be holy in all you do; for it is written: "Be holy, because I am holy."[26]

Created with attitudes

I have been trying to identify a godly person in recent days and I have a big challenge. Godliness in our time is known by how great a person preaches, how regular he or she goes to church, how much money such a person gives towards the work of God, how long and nicely he or she prays. All these are good but a tree is known by its fruits.

The other side of attitude

What is your attitude like? Whatever funny attitude you are exhibiting was not put there by default. Your change in attitude came as a virus when the tempter tempted our first parents. The good news is that Jesus took away all your sins on the cross and formatted your system, dealing with all the viruses that inhibited you from living the life you were created to live.

If you must show forth the glory of God. Your attitudes must show what stock you are made of. If people cannot connect with your creator because of

---

[26] 1 Peter 1:14-16. New International Version.

your attitudes, then you still need to be worked upon. I am not going to tell you who you are because you know who you are better than anyone else. Trying to pretend to be a good person will destroy you, and bring enmity with people around you, thereby thwarting the purpose to which you were created—to glorify him with your life.

Created for the Word

The Word of God is of optimal importance when it comes to glorifying the creator through worship. If you must live according to the creator's manual for your life, his word must be infused into everything you do. In fact, the Word itself says, *"That's the whole story. Here now is my final conclusion: Fear God and obey his commands, for this is everyone's duty."*[27] Another rendition of the Word puts it this way

All has been heard; the end of the matter is: Fear God [revere and worship Him, knowing that He is] and keep His commandments, for this is the whole of man [the full, original purpose of his creation, the object of God's providence, the root of character, the foundation of all happiness, the adjustment to all inharmonious circumstances

---

[27] Ecclesiastes 12:13. New Living Translation.

and conditions under the sun] *and* the whole [duty] for every man. [28]

I do not think I have any other explanation that is better than what is explained above. Keeping Gods commandment is actually obeying what he says. And what He says is captured in the Word—The Life Manual and you are duty-bound to obey his word.

A purifying agent

His Word is a lamp unto your feet, and a light unto your path. It should always direct you on how you should glorify God. When the Word hits you, it sanctifies you. The life manual says, "Sanctify them through thy truth: thy word is truth."[29] The truth of his word grants us the effrontery to face life challenges, knowing that his Word has answers to our daily events.

I am aware that it is becoming more and more challenging to listen to and read his Word because of the growing challenges to live with technology around us. I will like you to take advantage of the technology around you to gain access to his word. Take advantage of your phones, tablets, and

---

[28] Ecclesiastes 12:13. Amplified Bible
[29] John 17:17. King James Version.

computers to install Bible software that will keep you keep abreast with his Word at all times.

Created to give

The real Joy of enjoying your life is when you give from a true heart of love. Sometimes, acts of love seem more pleasant especially when you are giving out something that is very precious to you. At the end of the day, however, you become happy that you gave when you see the fruits of your giving. The things you do here on earth are being stored for you in your heavenly bank.

Friend, the life manual yet says:

> ...give to the needy. Provide yourselves with moneybags that do not grow old, with a treasure in the heavens that does not fail, where no thief approaches and no moth destroys. For where your treasure is, there will your heart be also.[30]

Bank deposit

You have a responsibility to love people and do acts of kindness to increase your heavenly bank account. The life manual says, *"Owe no one anything, except*

---

[30] Luke 12:33-34. English Standard Version.

to love each other, for the one who loves another has fulfilled the law."[31] Please keep loving and sharing the love of Christ through acts of kindness and in words.

Deposit confirmations

A time will come when you will stand before the creator and your works will speak for you. The life manual says of that day;

...the King will say to those on his right, 'Come, you who are blessed by my Father, inherit the kingdom prepared for you from the foundation of the world. For I was hungry and you gave me food, I was thirsty and you gave me drink, I was a stranger and you welcomed me, I was naked and you clothed me, I was sick and you visited me, I was in prison and you came to me.' Then the righteous will answer him, saying, 'Lord, when did we see you hungry and feed you, or thirsty and give you drink? And when did we see you a stranger and welcome you, or naked and clothe you? And when did we see you sick or in prison and visit you?' And the King will answer

---

[31] Romans 13:8. English Standard Version.

them, 'Truly, I say to you, as you did it to one of the least of these my brothers, you did it to me.'

The Bible further says:

Then he will say to those on his left, 'Depart from me, you cursed, into the eternal fire prepared for the devil and his angels. For I was hungry and you gave me no food, I was thirsty and you gave me no drink, I was a stranger and you did not welcome me, naked and you did not clothe me, sick and in prison and you did not visit me.' Then they also will answer, saying, 'Lord, when did we see you hungry or thirsty or a stranger or naked or sick or in prison, and did not minister to you?' Then he will answer them, saying, 'Truly, I say to you, as you did not do it to one of the least of these, you did not do it to me.' And these will go away into eternal punishment, but the righteous into eternal life.[32]

What can you do to glorify God through giving? You may just need to talk to someone who needs comfort. You could assist someone financially or go for medical missions. Hospitals and the prisons are

---

[32] Mathew 25:34-46. English Standard Version

looking for someone to visit, and the person to go visiting could be you. You may not really need to go too far to show an act of kindness. Look around, someone is waiting for your love. Take the step today, start thinking about it now!

6. Purpose for Living: Created for Relationships

We are afraid to care too much,
for fear that the other person
does not care at all.
-Eleanor Roosevelt

HUMAN BEINGS ARE RELATIONAL BEINGS; it is interwoven in our DNA to relate with each other. The creator himself saw this as a necessary part of human existence because he also related and relates as a triune being. It is therefore important to relate to Him as a person and to others cordially. The hunger in your heart to know and experience God in a personal way is planted there for a reason. The truth is, we were created to know him this way, to have a relationship with Him. The creator made us this way because He desired an intimate relationship with us before the beginning of time.[33]

Leverage in relationships

I have noticed that people who are relational get things done with more ease. Such people get the needed leverage in areas they are less capable of. If relationships are so important to human existence, why then are some people so proud of saying, "I do not relate much?" This could be because most of such people do not know they were created for relationships. In this chapter, I will try to look at specific areas of our human existence that need attention as per relationship. Note however, that all these relationships are and must be geared towards relating with and growing in Jesus.

Relationship: With the creator

I had earlier stated how our creator made the man and the woman in his own image. For the purpose of emphases, I will quote the same scripture again. The life manual says:

God spoke: "Let us make human beings in our image, make them reflecting our nature, so they

---

[33] Harland and Moser, *Seven Words of worship*. 7.

can be responsible for the fish in the sea, the birds in the air, the cattle, and, yes, Earth itself, and every animal that moves on the face of Earth." God created human beings; he created them godlike, Reflecting God's nature. He created them male and female.[34]

In His image

If you really want to understand the magnitude of why your Maker had to make you in his image, try to imagine relating with snakes, lions and other wild animals. Does it make sense? No, it does not. Of the truth, some people try to be close with some of these wild animals but it takes a lot of training, and so much risk is involved. Sometimes the true nature of those beasts shows up and the death of the human involved becomes a tragic result.

God made you in His own image for a relationship that will last forever. Harland and Moser elaborate this saying:

All lasting relationships are based on mutual interest, trust, and understanding. By choosing to create us in His image—with a mind (the ability to reason), a will and emotions—and by

---

[34] Genesis 1:26-27. The Message.

providing everything we need for life, God created and equipped us for a lasting relationship with Him.[35]

Like attract like

It is commonly said, "Birds of the same feather flock together." "like attract like." "Whatever you want, wants you." This exemplifies perfectly the law of homogenous attraction. [36] Being created in the image of God gravitates human beings towards him. This is why even animals of the same kind relate better with each other. God had to make us in his own image for a lasting relationship. All through the Bible—the Life manual makes it clear that God desires a relationship with you. He wants you closer to him in a personal way than you can ever imagine. These Bible quotes give a glimpse of this relationship I am talking about:

Where can I go from your Spirit? Where can I flee from your presence? If I go up to the heavens, you are there; if I make my bed in the depths, you are there. If I rise on the wings of the dawn, if I

---

[35] Harland and Moser, *Seven Words of worship.* 7.
[36] Brian Tracy. *The 100 absolutely unbreakable laws of business success,* (San Francisco: Berrett-Koehler publishers, inc, 2002), 22.

settle on the far side of the sea, even there your hand will guide me, your right hand will hold me fast. If I say, "Surely the darkness will hide me and the light become night around me," even the darkness will not be dark to you; the night will shine like the day, for darkness is as light to you.[37]

The intimate and organic relationship

What a mighty God we serve. If he is everywhere and nothing is hidden from him, rather than running away from his presence, I will rather do whatever it takes to enjoy his presence. The next quote says:

I am the Vine, you are the branches. When you're joined with me and I with you, the relation intimate and organic, the harvest is sure to be abundant. Separated, you can't produce a thing. Anyone who separates from me is deadwood, gathered up and thrown on the bonfire. But if you make yourselves at home with me and my words are at home in you, you can be sure that whatever you ask will be listened to and acted upon. This is how my Father shows who he is — when you produce grapes, when you mature as my

---

[37] Psalm 139:7-12. New International Version.

disciples. "I've loved you the way my Father has loved me. Make yourselves at home in my love.[38]

With him, there are all the benefits to enjoy. Tapping from the wealth of his being is more than I could ever hope for. The good news is; all he is asking is for me to abide in him. Sometimes it looks to me as if the whole God begs me for a relationship. While others are struggling to get to him, he instead came down for me, Wow!!! This relationship with him is not that he will just cast me away out of anger because I fail sometimes. He wants this intimate relationship to be continuous. Now listen to this:

Life from life

This is how we know we're living steadily and deeply in him, and he in us: He's given us life from his life, from his very own Spirit. Also, we've seen for ourselves and continue to state openly that the Father sent his Son as Savior of the world. Everyone who confesses that Jesus is God's Son participates continuously in an intimate relationship with God. We know it so well, we've embraced it heart and soul, this love that comes from God.[39]

---

[38] John 15:5-9. The Message.
[39] 1 John 4:13-16. The Message.

What else can I say, if my creator made me for a relationship with him, do I have any choice not to be relating to him? Others may choose otherwise but I will rather stick with the Bible and do exactly what I was created for—to have fellowship with him through his son Jesus Christ.

Relationship: With our families

Apart from my creator, my greatest asset in this world is my family. I love my family and I know that God put that love right down in my soul. Most troubled people and serial killers have their challenges from a lack of proper family upbringing. An ideal family begins with a married man and woman. A married man and man or married woman and woman are an aberration of the divine order.

Generated helpful relationship

God did create Adam and Eve primarily for relationships. When he saw the loneliness of man he said, "It's not good for the Man to be alone; I'll make him a helper, a companion.[40] This explains why a man leaves his father and mother and is joined to his

---

[40] Genesis 2:18. The Message.

wife, and the two are united into one."[41] This was and has been the creator's ideal for a family.

When a family is blessed with children, the creator expects such parents to take care of their children in all ways, he expects you to "direct your children onto the right path, and when they are older, they will not leave it.[42] This direction instructs all parents to know and understand their children.

Staying connected

God loves the unity in the family, you should, therefore, do all you can to stay connected. He says, "How wonderful, how beautiful, when brothers and sisters get along!"[43] It is a big challenge for siblings to get along. In some families, they even fight over irrelevant things but get back on track. Some do not for the rest of their lives.

Friend! Your family is very important and needs your attention. Yes, it is good to work to provide for your family. But remember, you were also made for relationship with your family. There must be a balance between your relationship with your family

---

[41] Genesis 2:24. New Living Translation.
[42] Proverbs 22:6. New Living Translation.
[43] Psalm 133:1. The Message.

and work. As a man, you cannot lazy around without providing for the family because you want to give them attention. Do you know why? The life manual says,

> If anyone fails to provide for his relatives, and especially for those of his own family, he has disowned the faith [by failing to accompany it with fruits] and is worse than an unbeliever [who performs his obligation in these matters].[44]

Balance work and family time

Relating well with your family includes providing for it. Do not say because you are not a man, you are absented. Work is God's creation and you must balance work and family time.

The creator also wants your family members to relate to him personally. You may be trusting him for a family member to be saved for a while but nothing is forthcoming. Do not be discouraged; they will surely come back home.

---

[44] 1 Timothy 5:8. Amplified Bible.

There was a man called Cornelius who lived in Caesarea, captain of the Italian Guards of the Bible times, Apostle Peter speaking about him said,

> ...he gave us an account of how he had seen the angel in his house, saying, Send to Joppa, and get Simon, named Peter, to come to you; Who will say words to you through which you and all your family may get salvation.[45]

Promised family rescue

Similarly, a jailer in desperation to be saved once asked Paul and Silas, "Sirs, what have I to do to get salvation? And they said, Have faith in the Lord Jesus, and you and your family will have salvation.[46] If God desired Cornelius and the jailer's families to be saved, your family is equally important and he will want them also saved.

Friend, do you think of your family as one of the reasons God created you to relate with, or you feel they are too unholy to be bothered about? If anything is hindering you from giving your family attention, please desist from such. It is possible that

---

[45] Acts 11:13-14. Bible in Basic English.
[46] Acts 16:30-31. Bible in Basic English.

you are too difficult for anyone to relate to. Be you a child, father or mother, the family is in the original plan of the creator and must be valued and cherished as such.

Relationship: With our friends

There are some friends that are truly a pain in the neck. Anytime you visit or they do, the aftermath of such a visit is a time of complaint to yourself, friends or family. Fortunately, and unfortunately, they are still there. Sometimes you wonder why you are still keeping such friends.

Friendship is not a competition

I have some people around me that all they do is to challenge whatever move I make. Somehow they think we are in some sort of competition. They are only motivated to do some certain things because they see me doing it. When they see me doing stuff or hear what I am about to do, they challenge it as a wrong move but shortly afterward you see them doing the same thing. They will never like or comment positively on your posts on social media except if they are challenging you.

There are some friends, however, whose work is to encourage you in whatever you do. They do not care if what you do is good or bad. All they care about is if you like it then do it. They can see you doing something terribly bad but as long as it is your choice, they will give you all the support to go ahead with your plans.

True friends are family

These kinds of friends that think they are competing with you are not true friends. The friends who also do not really care about what you do are also not good friends. The Life manual says, "There are "friends" who pretend to be friends, but there is a friend who sticks closer than a brother."[47] A true friend becomes like a family. In many cases, you are likely to share your personal challenges with true friends rather than family members. Your family also recognizes them as family. They would not pretend when you are doing the wrong thing. They point out your wrongs to you telling you to your face when you are going the wrong direction.

Now, if you seem to have friends that you do not ever disagree with, then someone is pretending. On

---

[47] Proverbs 18:24. The Living Bible.

the other hand, what is the point if you have friends and all that happens when you are around them is only painful experiences? They keep bullying you and you always keep mute because you do not want to hurt them. If you are keeping such friends, it is either you are taking advantage of the relationship, or you feel inferior, so hanging around them gives you a sense of belonging or you are merely unwise.

True friends disagree and agree

True friends will disagree to agree. Do not think that because you disagree with your friends so the relationship is necessarily bad. Sometimes you need to disagree, but keeping quiet because you do not want to hurt your friends is totally wrong. Your friends may cause you pain. Truly the scripture says, "Wounds from a friend are better than kisses from an enemy!"[48] Do not ever think that your friends hurt you so you will try an enemy. The love from your foe will lead you to doom. The kisses from your foe carry poison and in many cases, the time you realize the content of the honey-sweetness from such kisses, your doomsday is already there.

---

[48] Proverbs 27:6. The Living Bible.

This is the time to check if the people who seem to be doing you well, whom you consider as friends are actually your foe or friends.

Friend or foe

Your enemy is a person who feels hatred for, fosters harmful designs against, or engages in antagonistic activities against you; such a person is your adversary, foe, or opponent.[49] They may not show it openly but that does not change who they are.

The term enemy is originally derived from the Latin language for 'bad friend' (Latin: *inimicus*). The word enemy is strong. Anger, frustration, hatred, jealousy, envy, jealousy, fear and distrust are all emotions associated with the word enemy.

Your enemy will sometimes try to be close to you as much as possible to get a soft spot to strike you down. Remember, the Latin origin of the word enemy originated from a bad friend. It also says the emotions associated with your enemy are anger, hatred, frustration, envy, jealousy, fear, distrust, and respect that is grudging. If you notice such emotions

---

[49] Reference Dictionary, "Enemy," [cited July 30, 2015] Online:
https://www.dictionary.reference.com/browse/enemy.

from your friend, such a friend is a bad friend and therefore your enemy. If you keep pretending you do not know the person is your enemy and assume that it is only the devil that is your enemy, then consider such friends to be agents of the devil.

Signs of a good friend

Your friend, however, is the person who understands your history, believes in your future, and accepts you with no strings attached. Friends will come and go in your life, but more important than how long a friendship lasts is that a good friend will love you for who you are. Look at the big and small actions people you consider as friends take, if they prove your worth and do acts that show care then such people are surely your true friends.[50] Below are some common signs of a good friend.

i. Someone who will support you
ii. Someone you can trust and who would not judge you
iii. Someone who would not put you down or deliberately hurt your feelings
iv. Someone who is kind and has respect for you

---

[50] Reachout, "What makes a good friend," [cited July 30, 2015] Online: https://www.au.reachout.com/what-makes-a-good-friend.

v. Someone who will love you because they choose to, not because they feel like they should[51]

Other signs of a good friend include:

i. Someone whose company you enjoy
ii. Showing loyalty
iii. Being trustworthy and willing to tell you the truth, even when it's hard
iv. Someone who can laugh with you
v. Someone who is willing to stick around when things get tough
vi. Someone who makes you smile
vii. Someone who is there to listen
viii. Someone who will cry when you cry[52]

A set of different friendship rules

For Christians, friendship is slightly different. Santhosh confirms what I think of true friendship. A true friend is, therefore, the one who:[53]

---

[51] Reachout, "What makes a good friend," (cited 30 July, 2015).

[52] Reachout, "What makes a good friend," (cited 30 July, 2015).
[53] Most of the ideas of a true friend are from:

a. *Sympathizes and comforts:* If your friends are going through pain and difficulty, be part of their pain.

When three of Job's friends heard of all the tragedy that had befallen him, they got in touch with each other and traveled from their homes to comfort and console him.[54]

Unfortunately, their discussion with Job and their suggestions showed they were not true friends after all.

b. *Prays for his friend:* True friends pray for each other. Our prayers go a long way to wipe the tears of our friends. Your prayers will never be wasted. When you pray for your friends you attract your creator's blessings.

After Job had prayed for his three friends, the LORD made him prosperous again and gave him twice as much as he had had before. [55]

Santhosh, "Biblical Friendship - Who is a Friend?" [cited July 30, 2015] Online:
http://ccatenn.org/New_Creation/Articles/friend.asp.
[54] Job 2:11. The Living Bible.
[55] Job 42:10. Today's English Version.

c. *Forgives offense of his or her friend:* Friends will definitely offend you but that does not mean you should give up on them. It is important that you tell others about their mistakes. It is also equally important that you challenge your friends who are doing something wrong but never be in the habit of keeping people's records of wrong or sins. Because:

If you want people to like you, forgive them when they wrong you. Remembering wrongs can break up a friendship.[56]

d. *Loves at all times:* There are times you feel you should not show love to your friends, but,

"Friends love through all kinds of weather, and families stick together in all kinds of trouble." [57]

e. *Sticks closer than family:* The world teaches friendship as a convenience. If you are rich, and everything is going well, then you will have lots of friends. But the one who sticks to his friend in the time of need is a true friend.

---

[56] Proverbs 17:9. Today's English Version.
[57] Proverbs 17:17. The Message.

"Friends come and friends go, but a true friend sticks by you like family."[58]

f. *Can be trusted:* A true friend will be honest with you no matter what. There are people out there who will flatter you and exalt you to make you feel good even when you are going in the wrong direction, but a friend is one who sees through all that and speaks the truth. Sometimes we tend to enjoy flattery, but be careful of the flatterers, they are not your true friends.

"Wounds from a sincere friend are better than many kisses from an enemy."[59]

g. *Gives earnest counsel:* It is not every counsel that is beneficial. Some people never recovered from a single bad counsel given by a person they called their friend. A good friend will never give you counsel that will intentionally hurt you.

"Ointment and incense make the heart rejoice, likewise the sweetness of one's friend from sincere counsel."[60]

---

[58] Proverbs 18:24. The Message.
[59] Proverbs 27:6. New Living Translation.
[60] Proverbs 27:9 New English Translation.

h. *Lifts up:* There is an old proverb that says, "A friend in need is a friend indeed." This statement is absolutely true! We live in a world where people use and dump you when they think your usefulness is over. As bad as that is, everyone needs a friend. Scripture affirms this saying:

> You are better off to have a friend than to be all alone because then you will get more enjoyment out of what you earn. If you fall, your friend can help you up. But if you fall without having a friend nearby, you are really in trouble.[61]

i. *Gives:* There some friends who will allow you to tell them all your difficulties, and after you exhaust yourself, they will tell you how you need to have faith. The unfortunate thing about such friends is that you see them using money for things they should have sacrificed to meet your needs. It makes you remember the sacrifices you made for them. The time, money and energy you sacrifice for them when they are in need and feel cheated. A true friend will make efforts to give to their friends in need. The Bible paints the picture I have projected above as follows:

---

[61] Eccl 4:9-10. Contemporary English Version

Dear brothers, what's the use of saying that you have faith and are Christians if you aren't proving it by helping others? Will that kind of faith save anyone? If you have a friend who is in need of food and clothing, and you say to him, "Well, good-bye and God bless you; stay warm and eat hearty," and then don't give him clothes or food, what good does that do? So you see, it isn't enough just to have faith. You must also do good to prove that you have it. Faith that doesn't show itself by good works is no faith at all-it is dead and useless. [62]

Cut off the virus

Your Maker created you for relationships with friends but you have a responsibility to choose your friends. If you think you have people lurking around your life only for their advantage, it is high time you cut off some of those viruses you call your friends. Those people's only job is to corrupt, infest and infect you to a point that you no longer have control over your life.

Friend! You need to focus on those who really care about you. Not everybody can be your friend. Yes, it

---

[62] James 2:14-17. The Living Bible.

is true that you hold on to your real friends, but some of those friends that are like a virus to you must go. Please feel free to call it quit with them. Your relationship with them should only be based on leading them to God, but if doing this is taking you away from Him then you have to stay away completely. It is better that you glorify God and maintain a relationship with him than keeping your bad friends and missing out on God.

The co-Creator-Jesus spoke about his friendship to us saying:

> This is the very best way to love. Put your life on the line for your friends. You are my friends when you do the things I command you. I'm no longer calling you servants because servants don't understand what their master is thinking and planning. No, I've named you friends because I've let you in on everything I've heard from the Father.[63]

If there is a friend you need most, it is the co-Creator. He will never forsake you no matter the challenges you are going through. Other friends may be conditional friends but his friendship is

---

[63] John 15:13-15. The Message.

unconditional. He sticks close to you in all your difficulty and pain.

A void filled only by God

Joseph M. Scriven (1819-1896) had serious challenges in his life that would have made him give up on life. At 25 he was in love and to be married. The day before his wedding his fiancé died in a tragic drowning accident. The hurt in Joseph's life made him sail from his homeland to start a new life in Canada. While in Canada working as a teacher, he fell in love again and became engaged to Eliza Roche, a relative of one of his students. Once again, Joseph's hopes and dreams were shattered when Eliza became ill and died before the wedding could take place.

I have not gone through what Joseph had gone through but just imaging what he went through is causing pain in my heart. At this point, only his faith in God would have sustained him. Soon after Eliza's death, Joseph is said to have joined the Plymouth Brethren and began preaching for a Baptist church. He never married but spent the remainder of his life; giving all his time, money and even the clothes off his own back to help the less privileged and to spread the love and compassion of Jesus wherever he went.

Around the same time that Eliza died, Joseph received word from Ireland that his mother was ill. He could not go to be with her, so he wrote a letter of comfort and enclosed one of his poems entitled *What a Friend We Have in Jesus*. This poem has now become a popular hymn even in our days.

Yes, you were created for relationship with friends but the best option of a friend is Jesus. I'm guessing that Joseph's hymn can be a blessing to you as it has been to me and millions of people the world over.

What a Friend We Have in Jesus

What a Friend we have in Jesus, all our sins and griefs to bear!
What a privilege to carry everything to God in prayer!
O what peace we often forfeit, O what needless pain we bear,
All because we do not carry everything to God in prayer.

Have we trials and temptations? Is there trouble

anywhere?
We should never be discouraged; take it to the
Lord in prayer.
Can we find a friend so faithful who will all our
sorrows share?
Jesus knows our every weakness; take it to the
Lord in prayer.

Are we weak and heavy laden, cumbered with a
load of care?
Precious Savior, still our refuge, take it to the
Lord in prayer.
Do your friends despise, forsake you? Take it to
the Lord in prayer!
In His arms He'll take and shield you; you will
find a solace there.

Blessed Savior, Thou hast promised Thou wilt
all our burdens bear
May we ever, Lord, be bringing all to Thee in
earnest prayer.
Soon in glory bright unclouded there will be no
need for prayer
Rapture, praise and endless worship will be our
sweet portion there.[64]

---

64 Sharefaith. What a friend we have in Jesus the song and the
story," [cited July 30, 2015] Online:

While is great to have a friend in Jesus, you need to relate with people too. You may have been discouraged with friends and feel you cannot take it anymore? I believe God can bring the right people to you. You may also need to check your attitude. Do you love people and put your life on the line for them? Scripture encourages us to do so. It says, "This is the very best way to love. Put your life on the line for your friends."[65]

Relationship: Gods family

In many occasions, I develop a very close relationship with members of God's family without even knowing their tribe or where they come from until it becomes very necessary. I consider fellow Christians as members of the family. They are my true brothers and sisters with Jesus as my elder brother.

True family first

It is not partiality to give special attention to members of the family of God. The life manual says

---

visit http://www.sharefaith.com/guide/Christian-Music/hymns-the-songs-and-the-stories/what-a-friend-we-have-in-jesus-the-song-and-the-story.html.
[65] John 15:13. The Message.

we should "not get tired of well-doing; for at the right time we will get in the grain if we do not give way to weariness. So then, as we have the chance, let us do good to all men, and specially to those who are of the family of the faith."[66] It is commonly said "blood is thicker than water," referring to the relationship that is bound by blood and natural DNA, whereas the ultimate bonding blood should be that of Jesus.

I do not understand when people look at their fellow members of God's family like strangers. I have funny experiences where I visit a Christian and they are not moved to even offer me a drink, then a member of their natural blood family walks in, and for a moment I feel like trash. The same people who behaved as if they were sick or something, jump up to prepare a sumptuous meal for the person they consider as their true family member.

The question is who am I to such a person? Am I really related to such a person by the blood of Jesus which is higher than their natural family? I have long ago cut off from people who look at others as trash because they are not related to them by blood.

---

[66] Galatians 6:9-10. Bible in Basic English.

A shared life

What Christians need to know from God's Word in this regard is this. "if we walk in the light, God himself being the light, we also experience a shared life with one another..."[67] A sharing life in the family of God is also what we were created for. A person who sees his fellow Christian Brother or sister to be less important as compared to his or her natural family is misinformed.

The fellowship of God's family members is becoming more and more important as our times are becoming more perverse. This calls for true unity in the family of God, "Not giving up our meetings, as is the way of some, but keeping one another strong in faith..."[68]

I have noticed that people now prefer to tweet, chat, and do Facebook rather than have fellowship with one another. Sometimes you even take out time to visit a fellow brother or sister but the attention of the person is on his phone, computer or the television. Technology has cut off the fellowship we are supposed to give to people in God's family.

---

[67] 1 John 1:7. The Message.
[68] Hebrews 10:25. Bible in Basic English.

Family over entertainment

Many years ago, I was in Church on a Sunday morning worship service and we were supposed to come back for an evening service. That evening was one of those evenings when my country was playing a national football match. The pastor declared that the Word of God was very powerful that morning so all the Church members should use the rest of the day to meditate. The curiosity of a young man led me to the Pastor's house to see if he was really meditating. It was in the days when very few people had televisions in my nation. To my greatest surprise, the pastor's parlour was filled with Church members and neighbours watching the football match and screaming on top of their voices.

There is an evil in the land that has infested Christian homes, it is called entertainment. This evil comes in the name of movies, football, and every other sport, wrestling and all the entertainment out there too numerous to mention. Some of those different entertainments have cut you from having fellowship with one another, neglecting to even go for fellowship with other Christian believers.

Balancing technology and family time

Beloved! Some of those entertainments and technology are not bad in themselves. What you need to do is to give attention to your creator and people because they matter the most. See how you can live your life to incorporate technology in it, such that, rather than being a slave to technology, it should be of service to you.

You were created to be part of the family and you have the opportunity to be in God's family. Take advantage of this offer and live the life you were created to live—a part of God's family.

Relationship: The workplace

God is the originator of work; the whole process of creation was a lot of work. He took the time to create from one state to another. The Bible explains, "Heaven and Earth were finished, down to the last detail. By the seventh day, God had finished his work. On the seventh day he rested from all his work."[69] He started work and did it to the last details. If we must also get good results, we must pay attention to details as he did.

---

[69] Genesis 2:1-2. THE MESSAGE

The best for last

After doing the work of creation, God introduced his most priced creation to work.

> GOD took the Man and set him down in the Garden of Eden to work the ground and keep it in order."[70] There are some that are of the opinion that work is a curse. Such people tend to be lazy and give very little attention to their employers. You are advised to "Work hard at whatever you do. [Because] You will soon go to the world of the dead, where no one works or thinks or reasons or knows anything."[71]

If you understand that work is of God and that you were created to glorify your creator through the work you do, work will be more pleasurable. Work will even be better if you discover your individual purpose in life. I will, therefore, advise you to enjoy work and your workplace. If you, however, seem not to be enjoying your work and your workplace, there is a possibility that you are in the wrong place.

---

[70] Genesis 2:15. THE MESSAGE
[71] Ecclesiastes 9:10. Contemporary English Version.

Ed Silvoso has provided a thoughtful look at four types of Christians in the workplace in his book *Anointed for Business*. He cites the following four categories:

- Christian who is simply trying to survive.
- Christian who is living by Christian principles.
- Christian who is living by the power of the Holy Spirit.
- Christian who is transforming their workplace for Christ.[72]

Transforming the workplace

As a child of God, you should not just try to survive in the workplace or live by Christian principles. Trying to live by the power of the Holy Spirit in your workplace is good but not good enough. As a Christian, it is your responsibility to transform your workplace for the Lord. Here is what Jesus says about why you are on earth, and that includes the workplace.

---

[72] Ed Silvoso. "Anointed for Business," [cited July 30, 2015] Online:

http://www.intheworkplace.com/apps/articles/default.asp?articleid=12851&columnid=1935

Let me tell you why you are here. You're here to be salt-seasoning that brings out the God-flavors of this earth. If you lose your saltiness, how will people taste godliness? You've lost your usefulness and will end up in the garbage.

Here's another way to put it: You're here to be light, bringing out the God-colors in the world. God is not a secret to be kept. We're going public with this, as public as a city on a hill. If I make you light-bearers, you don't think I'm going to hide you under a bucket, do you? I'm putting you on a light stand. Now that I've put you there on a hilltop, on a light stand — shine! Keep open house; be generous with your lives. By opening up to others, you'll prompt people to open up with God, this generous Father in heaven.[73]

You are not on earth just to enjoy the money you make at work. Your workplace is your mission field. That is why I do not understand when people say they are full-time ministers of God. Such people in many cases consider bankers, engineers, doctors, civil servants and every other work that has no direct connection to preaching the word of God as below service. Every child of God is a fulltime

---

[73] Matthew 5:13-16. The Message.

minister of God in their workplace and they have a responsibility to be agents of transformation.

Diligence and fairness

The understanding of being agents of transformation should make you ask yourself at each point if you are glorifying God as an agent of transformation in your job. Both employees and employers must see work as a means of relating to God in a deeper way. The life manual emboldens:

Servants, do what is ordered by those who are your natural masters, having respect and fear for them, with all your heart, as to Christ; not only under your master's eye, as pleasers of men; but as servants of Christ, doing the pleasure of God from the heart; doing your work readily, as to the Lord, and not to men: In the knowledge that for every good thing anyone does, he will have his reward from the Lord, if he is a servant or if he is free. And, you masters, do the same things to them, not making use of violent words: in the knowledge that their Master and yours is in heaven, and he has no respect for a man's position.[74]

---

[74] Ephesians 6:5-9. Bible in Basic English.

God gives tributes to diligence and fairness. As an employer, you are called to be diligent and fair in your dealings! These are two great characteristics we are to have in the workplace. Thy are especially essential for the manager. Your creator hates it when people are exploited and he will surely judge all exploiters. So, rather than dishonesty and exploitation in the workplace, why don't you care for workers and encourage them to produce optimally?[75]

Working for better relationships

God created work and he expects you to relate well with your leaders, colleagues, and subordinates in a way that leads you to be the transforming agent you are. Work hard at your workplace to the glory of God This is because "Idle hands are the devil's workshop; idle lips are his mouthpiece."[76] I however, believe you were crafted not to be the devil's workshop or his mouthpiece. I am anticipating that someone out there will change their attitude towards work, and I am counting on you.

---

[75] Richard J. Krejcir, "How to Be a Christian in the Workplace," [cited July 30, 2015] Online: ww.discipleshiptools.org/apps/articles/default.asp?articleid= 41215.
[76] Proverbs 16:27. The living Bible.

Relationship: With the community

You are an individual who is born into a family, a nuclear family, and a community. Your life must be, therefore, felt positively in your community if you are a Christian. If your life is not positively impacting the people around you, then you are a misfit.

Call the shots

It is becoming more and more difficult to live as a Christian because the Church that is supposed to be setting the standards and calling the shots is failing in its responsibility. The church is gradually becoming worldly, so much so that there is hardly anything that is out there that has not rubbed off on the church. Apostle Paul admonishes as per relating to the society saying:

> ...here's what I want you to do, God helping you: Take your everyday, ordinary life — your sleeping, eating, going-to-work, and walking-around life — and place it before God as an offering. Embracing what God does for you is the best thing you can do for him. Don't become so well-adjusted to your culture that you fit into it without even thinking. Instead, fix your attention on God. You'll be changed from the inside out.

Readily recognize what he wants from you, and quickly respond to it. Unlike the culture around you, always dragging you down to its level of immaturity, God brings the best out of you, develops well-formed maturity in you. [77]

Do not let the community call the shots for you by squeezing you into its mould. Sometimes you may look odd because it seems you are doing things differently. Keep changing from the inside out as the Lord influences you to be the light and the salt that influences your community.

If you are already a believer in Jesus, I will like you to know that one of the reasons God did not call you to heaven is because he wants you to influence your community positively. So do not just be there without your neighbours having a full touch of your love. "Don't just pretend to love others. Really love them. Hate what is wrong. Hold tightly to what is good. Love each other with genuine affection, and take delight in honoring each other. "[78] this is a noble responsibility for the believer.

---

[77] Romans 12:1-2. The Message.
[78] Romans 12:9-10. New living Translation.

Loving difficult people

I must agree with you that is not easy to love everyone in your community. It is an uphill task to love some people who do not care you exist. I have met people who are so full of hate. An attempt to love them makes them feel suspicious. Some people hate you so much that even your attempt to maintain a relationship is rejected. You greet them and they do not respond. All they think of you is how they can get a nice spot to get a full pound of your flesh. The life manual advises that even with such people you should try to find beauty in them. It says,

> Don't hit back; discover beauty in everyone. If you've got it in you, get along with everybody. Don't insist on getting even; that's not for you to do. "I'll do the judging," says God. "I'll take care of it.[79]

This is a hard saying. I am personally struggling to relate with some people who I have tried to relate with them but hit the rock. You greet them and they do not respond, even when they do, they do it grudgingly. I will keep trying to the best of my abilities. So help me God.

---

[79] Romans 12:17-19. The Message.

You cannot live in isolation

Now, just so that you will not misunderstand me. All I am trying to say here is that you cannot live in isolation to your community. You must befriend your community for the reason of pointing community members to Christ. If you live in a community and people are not sure you are a Christian, then you need to give attention to your life and work your way to relate with your community as the Bible expects you to.

Relationship: With the government

There is a funny way some devoted Christians think. They think that service to the church is so important that any other authority does not deserve the kind of respect they give to the church. They forget that the Bible says:

Everyone must submit to governing authorities. For all authority comes from God, and those in positions of authority have been placed there by God. So anyone who rebels against authority is rebelling against what God has instituted, and they will be punished. For the authorities do not strike fear in people who are doing right, but in those who are doing wrong. Would you like to live without fear of the authorities? Do what is right, and they will honor you. The authorities are God's servants, sent for your good. But if you are doing wrong, of course you should be afraid, for they have the power to punish you. They are God's servants, sent for the very purpose of punishing those who do what is wrong. So you must submit to them, not only to avoid punishment, but also to keep a clear conscience.

Pay your taxes, too, for these same reasons. For government workers need to be paid. They are serving God in what they do. Give to everyone what you owe them: Pay your taxes and government fees to those who collect them, and give respect and honor to those who are in authority.[80]

Obeying constituted authority

The nonchalant activities toward the government are not of God. If the creator is the person who puts government in place, disobedience to constituted authority violates his word. We are expected to relate well with the government. We are further admonished to:

---

[80] Romans 13:1-7. New Living Translation.

Pray especially for rulers and their governments to rule well so we can be quietly about our business of living simply, in humble contemplation. This is the way our Savior God wants us to live.[81]

The responsibility of the church is not unnecessary criticism of the government but to pray and get involved wherever necessary. It is bad for Christians to fold their hands and watch other destroy constituted Government authority. They must also get involved politically and otherwise.

Never forget that God created you for his own glory and for relationships. But he also created you for service. In the next chapter, we will see how you can make the most of your service to God in diverse ways.

---

[81] 1 Timothy 2:2-3. The Message.

7. Purpose for Living: Created for Service

Always render more and better
service than is expected of you,
 no matter what your task may be.
-Og Mandino

IF YOU ARE A CHRISTIAN, YOU ARE automatically a minister— called to ministry, created for ministry, saved for ministry, and gifted for ministry. As Rick Warren will say, not every Christian is a pastor or can be a pastor, but every Christian is a minister because to be like Christ is to be a minister as he did and does. You cannot be like Jesus Christ without serving others as he did.[82]

---

[82] Rick Warren. "What on earth am I here for?" [cited July 30, 2015] Online:
 https://pastors.com/what-on-earth-am-i-here-for/.

Called to serve

The word "Ministry" or to minister is from the Greek word *diakoneo*, meaning "to serve" or *douleuo*, meaning "to serve as a slave." The New Testament, however, sees ministry as service to God and to humanity in the name of God. Jesus our servant-leader provided the pattern for Christian ministry— He came not to be served but to serve. We are therefore saved to serve.[83] In the saviour's very words he says:

> ...Whoever wants to be great must become a servant. Whoever wants to be first among you must be your slave. That is what the Son of Man has done: He came to serve, not be served — and then to give away his life in exchange for the many who are held hostage."[84]

He went ahead and practically demonstrated this service in a very dramatic and humble manner. The life manual records this as follows:

---

[83] Gotquestions, "What is Christian ministry?" [cited July 30, 2015] Online: https://www.gotquestions.org/what-is-ministry.html.
[84] Mathew 20:26-28. The Message.

After Jesus had washed his disciples' feet and had put his outer garment back on, he sat down again. Then he said:

Do you understand what I have done? You call me your teacher and Lord, and you should, because that is who I am. And if your Lord and teacher has washed your feet, you should do the same for each other. I have set the example, and you should do for each other exactly what I have done for you. I tell you for certain that servants are not greater than their master, and messengers are not greater than the one who sent them. You know these things, and God will bless you, if you do them.[85]

The Co-Creator Jesus set the example of service for us to follow. He is a perfect example of a servant-leader. In this chapter, we will look at the different areas of service you were created for.

---

[85] John 13:12-17 Contemporary English Version.

Service to our lives

Great people the world over are involved in works of service. Many of them have a great name and have blessed a lot of people. As great as their service are, the greatest disservice some of them are doing is neglecting their soul. Jesus says:

> ...If any of you wants to be my follower, you must turn from your selfish ways, take up your cross, and follow me. If you try to hang on to your life, you will lose it. But if you give up your life for my sake and for the sake of the Good News, you will save it. And what do you benefit if you gain the whole world but lose your own soul?[86]

The most important need

No matter the great works of service a person does, no matter how much a person makes before people, if such a person does not give attention to denying self and connecting with the saviour, such philanthropy is useless. Because of the importance of eternity, we need to keep watch over our lives as people of old did.

---

[86] Mark 8:34-36. New Living Translation.

Apostle Paul is very particular about safe-guarding himself jealously for a higher price. This he says:

> Do you not know that in a race all the runners compete, but [only] one receives the prize? So run [your race] that you may lay hold [of the prize] and make it yours.

> Now every athlete who goes into training conducts himself temperately and restricts himself in all things. They do it to win a wreath that will soon wither, but we [do it to receive a crown of eternal blessedness] that cannot wither.

> Therefore, I do not run uncertainly (without definite aim). I do not box like one beating the air and striking without an adversary.

> But [like a boxer] I buffet my body [handle it roughly, discipline it by hardships] and subdue it, for fear that after proclaiming to others the Gospel and things pertaining to it, I myself should become unfit [not stand the test, be unapproved and rejected as a counterfeit].[87]

---

[87] 1 Corinthians 9:24-27 Amplified Bible.

Death is the answer

The challenge to keep fit spiritually is not to be taken for granted. Yes! You have a responsibility to serve, but first things first. Take care of yourself. The best way to do this is to let yourself go. Paul discovered this secret and says:

> Christ's life showed me how, and enabled me to do it. I identified myself completely with him. Indeed, I have been crucified with Christ. My ego is no longer central. It is no longer important that I appear righteous before you or have your good opinion, and I am no longer driven to impress God. Christ lives in me. The life you see me living is not "mine," but it is lived by faith in the Son of God, who loved me and gave himself for me. I am not going to go back on that...[88]

Wow! It is a challenging life to live, that is why a Paul will face death face to face and say he dies daily. The greatest service you will do to yourself is to be in a relationship with Jesus and hang in there by his grace on a daily basis. Do not forget, he is interested in your character. He wants you to be more and more like him, for this is how you were

---

[88] Galatians 2:20-21. The Message.

created to be. "God is far more interested in what you are than in what you do. He's far more interested in your being than in your doing."[89] Any service that that does not start with this service to your life by connecting with and staying with Jesus to transform your life is misappropriated.

Service to God

The life manual says, "In the beginning God..." For me, this indicates that he is the beginning and the end. I have connected with him and he has never disappointed me. Remember that you were created for his glory, for relationships, and for service. I therefore, stand on the foundation of his Word together with Paul to implore you saying, "Dear friends, God is good. So I beg you to offer your bodies to him as a living sacrifice, pure and pleasing. That's the most sensible way to serve God."[90] I believe that your sensibility will make you make the right choice.

---

[89] Rick Warren. "What on earth am I here for?" (cited 30 July, 2015).

[90] Romans 12:1. Contemporary English Version.

Respect and obedience

I am not about to tell you insensible ways to serve God. One thing I know however is that offering yourself to him is a sensible way of service. It will be in your best interest if you obey him to offer yourself to his service. His Word says, "Everything you were taught can be put into a few words: Respect and obey God! This is what life is all about."[91] The question here could be, "how much do you obey him?—His Word and personal instructions. Do you really know that life is all about respect and obedience to God? if you did not know, now you know and you need to do something about it.

There are things His Word instructs all Christians to obey; while other services are specific to you. When you do not do them, even though you are not particularly sinning, you carry guilt around.

Service by default

You have a responsibility to serve him by default. When you choose to disobey him on purpose, you chose to fail. Could your creator be reminding you

---

[91] Ecclesiastes 12:13. Contemporary English Version.

right now of a service he has asked you to do and you have been running away? Your life is all about respect and obedience to God. Make sure you do not malfunction as a result of disobedience. Stay with the original program God installed in your DNA—obedience.

Service to our families

He created you in a family, even if you never got to know your birth-parents, you are still a family. I took the time to explain that a person who does not provide for his family is worse than an unbeliever. Actually, this is what the Bible says. There are other services you are required to give your family that may seem simple. They are, however, very important for the bond in the family. You may just need to be more available for your family, play or go out with your family some more, or you could just need to live the example your family needs to follow.

The little services matter

I want to believe that, somehow you have an idea of how you need to serve your family. You have been having promptings to do things differently. The question is "why can't you just go ahead and give that service to your family?" Don't you know your life will be a lot better if you live together in unity and give your family the desired service? All you may need to do could be to do dishes or do the garden, do school runs, or some other minor house chores and the needed love in your family will come.

Below is a hymn from Proverbs 31:10-31 of the kind of woman that gives service to her family. This ideal woman can be a man. Do not think that because it talks about a woman so it is not referring to men also.

Hymn to a Good Wife

A good woman is hard to find, and worth far more than diamonds.
Her husband trusts her without reserve, and never has reason to regret it.
Never spiteful, she treats him generously all her life long.

She shops around for the best yarns and cottons, and enjoys knitting and sewing.

She's like a trading ship that sails to faraway places and brings back exotic surprises.

She's up before dawn, preparing breakfast for her family and organizing her day.

She looks over a field and buys it, then, with money she's put aside, plants a garden.

First thing in the morning, she dresses for work, rolls up her sleeves, eager to get started.

She senses the worth of her work, is in no hurry to call it quits for the day.

skilled in the crafts of home and hearth, diligent in homemaking.

She's quick to assist anyone in need, reaches out to help the poor.

She doesn't worry about her family when it snows; their winter clothes are all mended and ready to wear.

The hymn further says

She makes her own clothing, and dresses in colorful linens and silks.

Her husband is greatly respected when he deliberates with the city fathers.
She designs gowns and sells them, brings the sweaters she knits to the dress shops.

Her clothes are well-made and elegant, and she always faces tomorrow with a smile.

When she speaks she has something worthwhile to say, and she always says it kindly.

She keeps an eye on everyone in her household, and keeps them all busy and productive.

Her children respect and bless her; her husband joins in with words of praise:
"Many women have done wonderful things, but you've outclassed them all!"
Charm can mislead and beauty soon fades.
The woman to be admired and praised is the woman who lives in the Fear-of-GOD.
Give her everything she deserves!
Festoon her life with praises! [92]

---

92 Proverbs 31:10-31. The Message.

Service to God's family

The church of God is not just an organization but an organism. A strong entity that requires all hands to be on deck for proper functionality. To properly understand the operation of this body and family of God, is to know what His Word says about it. And this is what it says:

> ...The only accurate way to understand ourselves is by what God is and by what he does for us, not by what we are and what we do for him.

> In this way we are like the various parts of a human body. Each part gets its meaning from the body as a whole, not the other way around. The body we're talking about is Christ's body of chosen people. Each of us finds our meaning and function as a part of his body. But as a chopped-off finger or cut-off toe we wouldn't amount to much, would we? So since we find ourselves fashioned into all these excellently formed and marvelously functioning parts in Christ's body, let's just go ahead and be what we were made to be, without enviously or pridefully comparing ourselves with each other, or trying to be something we aren't.

If you preach, just preach God's Message, nothing else; if you help, just help, don't take over; if you teach, stick to your teaching; if you give encouraging guidance, be careful that you don't get bossy; if you're put in charge, don't manipulate; if you're called to give aid to people in distress, keep your eyes open and be quick to respond; if you work with the disadvantaged, don't let yourself get irritated with them or depressed by them. Keep a smile on your face.[93]

No role is inferior

There is no way you can say you do not have anything to offer in this family. Everyone has a role to play, and every role is important. Do not also think your role is inferior to the other person, and do not think because people are flocking around you, so your role is greater than the person who does his or her duty in quietness. You cannot also do everything either. Free your hands if you discover that your service is not a call but a necessity. Doing some things out of necessity should just be for a while. At a point the apostle's hands were full and this is what they did.

---

[93] Romans 12:3-8. The Message.

So the Twelve called a meeting of the disciples. They said, "It wouldn't be right for us to abandon our responsibilities for preaching and teaching the Word of God to help with the care of the poor. So, friends, choose seven men from among you whom everyone trusts, men full of the Holy Spirit and good sense, and we'll assign them this task. Meanwhile, we'll stick to our assigned tasks of prayer and speaking God's Word."

The congregation thought this was a great idea. They went ahead and chose... Then they presented them to the apostles. Praying, the apostles laid on hands and commissioned them for their task.[94]

You cannot do everything

There are some members of God's family that are never satisfied with anything and anybody. This is a body and it must function as a body by integrating with each part. If done otherwise, there will be a serious malfunction. It is possible that many of the challenges we have in the church are because some believers are seeming to do everything. This kind of

---

[94] Acts 6:2-6. The Message.

operation cannot bring the desired unity we seek in the body of Christ.

The early church's operation gives us an example of how a church should function to meet people's physical and material needs. The Bible says:

> The whole group of believers was united in their thinking and in what they wanted. None of them said that the things they had were their own. Instead, they shared everything. With great power the apostles were making it known to everyone that the Lord Jesus was raised from death. And God blessed all the believers very much. None of them could say they needed anything. Everyone who owned fields or houses sold them. They brought the money they got and gave it to the apostles. Then everyone was given whatever they needed.[95]

Their service is challenging

Unfortunately, individualism is becoming the order of the church. People are more concerned with themselves and hardly look out for one another's needs. I see people who have a false idea of God.

---

[95] Acts 4:32-35. Easy-to-Read Version.

They give and serve members of their religion with all vigour. They also do some philanthropic feat, yet many Christians have unfortunately not decided to serve the church until they are cajoled into service.

If you are of God, you are my Brother or Sister because you are the family of God. Your call to service into God's household is purposed by design. Go ahead and do your bit even if it does not attract attention. What is important is that you did the service from a sincere heart.

Service to humanity

Your purpose by design is to love and care for people, even if they do not care about you. They may antagonize you and give no attention to your service for them. The Word of God yet urges us to do good to them saying:

Wish only good for those who treat you badly. Ask God to bless them, not curse them. When others are happy, you should be happy with them. And when others are sad, you should be sad too. Live together in peace with each other. Don't be proud, but be willing to be friends with people who are not important to others. Don't think of yourself as smarter than everyone else.[96]

Philanthropy is of God

Our Maker tells us to bless and love people, whether they are happy or sad. I see this going on in Africa and other developing nations. The government and other Non-Governmental Organizations are doing what they can to help people in need. It, however, baffles me that, some people are having NGO's just to raise funds and misappropriate it. They care more about using the monies for themselves rather than what they raised it for.

Philanthropic movements did not start today. The life manual tells us about a woman who was a philanthropist, and her humanitarian service was felt by people in her community. The Bible records her humanitarian services as follows:

Now there was in Joppa a disciple named Tabitha, which, translated, means Dorcas. She was full of good works and acts of charity. In those days she became ill and died... the disciples, hearing that Peter was there, sent two

---

96 Romans 12:14-16. Easy-to-Read Version.

men to him... And when he arrived, they took him to the upper room. All the widows stood beside him weeping and showing tunics and other garments that Dorcas made while she was with them.[97]

What will you be remembered for?

If I may ask, what will you be remembered for? Dorcas was remembered for the service she did in her community. When people think about you, do they think about the good things you do or they remember every evil you have done to them and society? Your pious life without getting involved in people's material and financial needs will be inconsequential. The scripture lauds this way:

Dear friends, do you think you'll get anywhere in this if you learn all the right words but never do anything? Does merely talking about faith indicate that a person really has it? For instance, you come upon an old friend dressed in rags and half-starved and say, "Good morning, friend! Be clothed in Christ! Be filled with the Holy Spirit!" and walk off without providing so much as a coat or a cup of soup — where does that get you?

---

[97] Acts 9:36-39. English Standard Version.

Isn't it obvious that God-talk without God-acts is outrageous nonsense? [98]

Actions above speech

It is high time we began to talk with our actions rather than speech. Though it is totally great to do service to humanity by giving our material and financial content, the greatest service anyone can do to humanity is to lead people to Christ—to do the work of missions.

Before the saviour went back to heaven after his earthly ministry, he gave his departing speech instructing us to lead people to him. His Word says:

> ...I have been given all authority in heaven and on earth! Go to the people of all nations and make them my disciples. Baptize them in the name of the Father, the Son, and the Holy Spirit, and teach them to do everything I have told you. I will be with you always, even until the end of the world.[99]

There is no greater service to humanity than for a person to give others direction to God. Making

---

[98] James 2:14-17. The Message.
[99] Mathew 28:18-20. Contemporary English Version.

disciples is our responsibility as Christians to our generation. Discipleship is the best means available for people to grow to be like Christ. Going out for missions and evangelism is one thing, discipleship is another. The greatest service that surpasses physical gifts to people is, therefore, missions and discipleship. This does not mean philanthropy is out of place.

Service for the ecology

The proper functionality and harmony of the ecological community and its environment is what is called the ecosystem. When a part of the system begins to malfunction, the ecosystem suffers. God is responsible for the harmony and the teamwork behind the ecosystem, and he has put humans in charge of making sure that the earth is properly taken care of.

When one or other parts of the ecosystems begin to function divergently due to human neglect or the seeming natural disaster caused by the mistreatment of the earth, serious consequences are likely to take place.

Nations the world over are talking and trying to tackle the challenge of global warming as a result of the depletion and disharmony of the ozone layer.

The relevance of caring for the earth cannot be overemphasized when it comes to the proper functionality of the ecosystem.

Responsible for His creation

The care for ecology is as old as the early days of creation. In fact, one of the first responsibilities God gave humans was to take care of creation. When He made every other thing he said:

> ...Let us make human beings in our image, make them reflecting our nature so they can be responsible for the fish in the sea, the birds in the air, the cattle, and, yes, Earth itself, and every animal that moves on the face of Earth." God created human beings; he created them godlike, Reflecting God's nature. He created them male and female. God blessed them: "Prosper! Reproduce! Fill Earth! Take charge! Be responsible for fish in the sea and birds in the air, for every living thing that moves on the face of Earth."[100]

---

[100] Genesis 1:26-28. The Message.

In another account of creation, the life manual gives other details of the creations as follows: The Creator...

> ...took dust from the ground and made a man. He breathed the breath of life into the man's nose, and the man became a living thing. Then the LORD God planted a garden in the East, in a place named Eden. He put the man he made in that garden... to work the soil and take care of the garden.[101]

Treating creation with the utmost respect

In the quotes above, it is established that the responsibility of taking care of the environment is a duty that God has given to all human beings. The challenge, however, is our nonchalant attitudes towards the environment. Dillon Burroughs in amazement as to the Christian responsibility to the environment says:

> For those of us who call ourselves Christians, how are we to treat things God calls good? The simple answer is that we better care a lot about what God calls good. God called people "good," animals

---

[101] Genesis 2:7,8, 15. Easy-to-Read Version.

"good," and a whole list of virtues, the church, and especially His Son Jesus "good." We are called to treat these areas of life with the utmost respect. Why would we treat the environment any differently? [102]

If we must take care of the environment, we must understand how to. Through study, I have discovered tons of ways to take care of the environment. I have also noticed that non-Christian groups seem to be giving more attention to environmental sustainability. Instead of giving you fifty ways of how to maintain the environment. I will give you the **5-Re's** of taking care of the environment I adopted from patheos [103] and adjusted to fit my context.

The 5-Re's of environmental care

a. *Reduce:* The truth is that we create LOTS of trash. I was involved in a research on how much trash is generated in Abuja and I was shocked

---

[102] Dan King. "5 Ways You Can Care for the Environment," [cited July 30, 2015] Online:
https://www.patheos.com/blogs/thehighcalling/2015/04/glo bal-care-activist-faith/.
[103] King. "5 Ways You Can Care for the Environment," (cited 30 July, 2015).

that even in my country, so much trash is produced. Be creative in reducing trash, please.

b. *Reuse:* If we can get over always "needing" brand new on everything it will help the environment. Reusing stuff does not necessarily mean you cannot afford to use new ones, it simply means you are responsible for the environment. When we reuse, we decrease the need to produce more, which only creates more potential waste.

c. *Recycle:* This is one of the simplest ways to reduce the amount of trash we create. Not only does this reduce the need to use up limited natural resources, but it can also save energy. The other good thing about recycling stuff is that you can exchange them for cash.

d. *Rethink:* Think through every aspect of your life. How much energy you use or trash you produce. Use energy-saving bulbs and switch off light and computers if you are not using them. Think of giving out your old stuff for others to use. Think about avoiding indiscriminate bush burning. Think about reducing the number of machines and cars you use. Sometimes you just need to walk rather than using your car. Just rethink on several other ways to sustain the environment. You can check the internet or buy a book on environmental sustainability.

e. *Replant:* This step is about replenishing the resources which have been depleted over the years. It may not be as extreme in some areas, but there are many developing nations with severe deforestation issues (which creates other problems too). So do not simply stop the cycle, let us reverse it too.

I am glad to be part of maintaining the environment. I am glad that he created me for this. Do all you can to be of service to yourself, to God, to the community, to the government, and to the environment. Never forget, "The earth belongs to God! Everything in all the world is his! He is the one who pushed the oceans back to let dry land appear."[104]

---

[104] Psalm 24:1-2. The Living Bible

8. Purpose Personalized

If you have a strong purpose in
life, you don't have to be pushed.
Your passion will drive you there.
-Roy T. Bennett,

MAY I REMIND YOU WHAT MY PEOPLE say, *"Shawon ka ruam man nyam."* Roughly translated, "Our purpose for living is to eat". This saying may have held meaning in the days of our forefathers but it currently lacks value. Our purpose on earth is beyond merrymaking and jamborees.[105] This brings us to the question, "what was I really created on earth for?" In the last three chapters, I took the time to explain how you were created for God's glory, relationships, and for his service. This service also extends to fellow

---

[105] Shadrach Loho-u-Ter. *Tripartite Battlegrounds* (Gboko: Freelife Press and Publishers, 2014), 23.

humans and the ecology. Knowing your general purpose of living is a step further to help you discover your individual purpose in life.

Beyond hype

The hype of knowing our purpose in life has made people do a lot of weird things to discover who they are. Some people have left their home countries to faraway lands for some form of meditation in monasteries, yet the searches seem to be unending. Others who have gone for a pilgrimage to Mecca, Jerusalem, and other places just to discover a deeper emptiness.

There are a few things however that you need to do to discover your life purpose. This process is very simple but you must believe it works.

Purpose probing check

i. Take a piece of paper and write down ten things you like doing.
ii. Adjust your list to select the five things you enjoy most.
    Are the five things you have chosen among the first three you wrote?

iii. From the five things, select the three things you know you are good at.

iv. Do other people also say you are good in the three areas you have selected?

v. Among the three things you have selected, which one will you do with excitement as free voluntary service without complaints?

vi. Crosscheck your heart if your last choice gives you peace and joy.

vii. Ask your friends and family if they notice your last choice is giving you peace and joy.

viii.   Try to volunteer your service for free and see if what you are doing is giving you joy.

ix. Crosscheck to see if your choice glorifies God, and is improving your relationship with him (God) and other people. Also find out if your choice is of service to God, the community, and the environment.

x. If you have come to the end of the test and you got what gives you excitement the most, then that should be your personal life purpose.

Everyone has a purpose

Our uniqueness has given each person special responsibilities in this life as per their purpose. I had watched an Indian movie called, "The three idiots" and heard this quotation, "make your passion your career and work becomes a play." I wish I had the power to tell you who you should be, but I do not. No matter who tells you who you should be; the job to discover your purpose in life can only be determined by you. Your current job may only be the means or the path to your individual purpose. Everyone on earth has an individual purpose and you cannot be an exception.[106]

I hope the test above, helped you to discover your individual purpose for living. If it did, which I know it will. Hold tight to it even if it seems not to be as lucrative as people expect it to be.

Maybe I should give you an idea of how I discovered my life purpose. I hope my story can help affirm the choice you have made in the purpose diagnosis test you took above.

How I discovered my purpose

When I was growing up, I discovered that I loved drawing, dancing, acting drama, singing, and doing anything with my hands that required me to think creatively. I also discovered that I loved speaking. In my secondary school, the school administration

---

[106] Loho-u-Ter Shadrach, *Tripartite Battlegrounds*, 25.

chose me to be transferred to a technical school after my Junior Secondary School because of my creativeness in fine arts. When I went to the technical school, I was sent to the carpentry and joinery department. After the technical school, I began to work with an architectural firm because of my skills in technical drawing. From there I went to read Fine and Applied Arts at the ordinary diploma level. Meanwhile, in the process of schooling, I was almost all the time selected to teach and be in leadership everywhere I went. Sometimes as a class representative, an elder in the church, or in some groups I belonged to.

I also volunteered

Several years passed and I discovered myself in a job that required me to teach people around the country. Before this job, I volunteered to do short term missions with Calvary ministries—CAPRO without pay. I used my fine art skills to develop awareness materials while I was with CAPRO. Up till now, my experience in Calvary Ministries is what I will ever thank God for.

My ability to teach

All these experiences were leading me somewhere I could say is my Purpose for living. When I finally began to School in the seminary, the learning environment was completely different from the background I had to be a hands-on-man. Then I discovered that my creative skills began to show in the way I wrote. My lecturers quickly discovered my ability to teach and the assigned me to teach Graphics and Teaching Aids while I was an undergraduate student. I was in the education department where my teaching skills further improved tremendously.

You see, I am a creative person and I love to talk. My creativity led me not just to dance, draw, or act creatively but to also think, lead, and write creatively. I have discovered that over the years, my various skills were there to harness my individual purpose for living. I now consider myself not just a life coach but a coach-leader. My various creative skills help me to teach in a psychomotor (practical) way. In many cases, when I teach people, they hardly forget because of my teaching style.

The emergence of a life coach

I am obsessed with developing people through my various leadership roles, and I channel all my skills into it. I have now resorted to writing and teaching people. That is why I opted for a Ph.D. in Educational Leadership and Administration in the first place.

When I put posts on social media, unconsciously, most of the posts are targeted on improving people. You can call me a teacher, a trainer, an inspirational speaker, a preacher, an author, a pioneer or a coach. But you will quickly discover that all these are encapsulated with my creative and teaching skills. All these help me to develop people holistically—spirit, soul, and body. This is my individual purpose for living, if you will want me to put my purpose in a sentence, it will be something like this. *"To lead people to a life of holistic abundance through writing and teaching."* I was created to lead, write, train, and coach people. That is why I am a life coach and coach-leader. Any other options on my path to destiny are purpose retardants.

Purpose must not be sophisticated

It will be terrible for any person to go through life without discovering his or her purpose and maximizing it. People like King David died in peace because they accomplished their purpose for living. Now, hear the testimony about him. The Bible says "For David, after he had served the purpose of God in his own generation, fell asleep and was laid with his fathers..."[107] May your purpose never be cut short. Make sure you do all the thinking and asking to discover it. Like I said, your purpose does not have to look sophisticated like the other person. Follow it as long as it gives you joy and peace.

---

[107] Acts 13:36-37. English Standard Version.

9. Conclusion

The end of all knowledge
should be service to others."
-Cesar Chavez

A tale of courage

MY SON SHALMAN WAS FULL OF LIFE AS he grew. As the manner of children is, he wanted to be everything—Teacher, pilot, aeronautic engineer, musician, pastor and a whole lot of things. Very intelligent yet he was not performing optimally in class. The career guidance in his school thought he should do arts. Shalman, however, thought he was better in the sciences. At that point, he struggled to pass his exams. Sometimes I got discouraged but I remembered how I never discovered my purpose in secondary school and maintained my calm.

He chose his convictions

When he was to be promoted to the senior secondary school, he was posted to the art class. After one year of doing arts, he was dissatisfied with everything. We had to have a roundtable talk to discuss his career. He chose to repeat the Senior Secondary School class (SS1), so he would study in the science classes. We obliged and change his school to a special science school. He struggled all though but he was determined to follow his heart. We had to meet one of his school guardians Mr. John Tsavnum for counsel. He advised us to be calm and wait for the final examination. True to it, when he wrote his West African Examination Council—WAEC exams, he passed with three distinctions, three credits, and one pass.

The diagnosis works

Before Shalman graduated from secondary school, I wrote the first manuscript of the purpose of living in 2015. I tested it on him and the diagnosis pointed him to computer science and music. Very weird combination right? I just kept to mind my findings. At this point, he never composed a song as far as I knew. What I did, however, was to encourage him to follow his heart, and he did.

As of now, Shalman is already participating in talent hunts and singing on live radio programs. He also got admission to read Computer Science Education at the University of Jos. The purpose diagnosis worked on him. He is a happier person because he knows exactly what he was created for and he is doing it. I see him growing and becoming a great person as he continues in his vision.

Everyone has the
right to be happy

I have also tested the purpose diagnosis on Godwin and Sharon, my other children. They choose their careers based on the test. I will not talk much about them because I am observing if they will follow through on the test. Meanwhile, they seem to be happy with their choices.

The choices you make in line with your purpose will make you a happy person. They may not be huge or attractive in the eyes of other people but they will make you happy. While everyone in this world may not be financially rich, everyone has the right to be happy. The choice to be happy is synonymous with discovering one's purpose. That is why this book is very important and doing the test in the preceding chapter is ideal.

Vital reminders

You have come a long way and it is time you stopped here, and read the other books in this series. Just before you drop the book, I will like to remind you that people will try to make choices for you but only you can determine who you are. They are many purpose retardants on your way to destiny; make sure they do not keep you away from your destiny.

Remember, you were created for God's glory, for relationship, and for service. You must have discovered your personal purpose in the last chapter. Harness it with the tripartite life purposes and your life will enjoy bliss in unusual ways. Apostle Paul understood the crucial nature of his purpose for living and said.

> But I do not consider my life of any account as dear to myself, so that I may finish my course and the ministry which I received from the Lord Jesus, to testify solemnly of the gospel of the grace of God.[108]

---

[108] Acts 20:24 New American Standard Bible (Updated)

Bliss for Paul was beyond what he will eat, where he will sleep, and what he will put on his body. It was all about fulfilling his call for ministry; which was his primary purpose for living. Purposeful living is a life of honour guided by God. It is the best life to live be it convenient or not, joy accompanies it.

Looking inward and upward

While people should confirm your purpose, do not look at them as the primary source to know your purpose. Look inward and upward and you will be happy you did. May you never miss out on the intent of why God made you. You are made for greatness, do not try to fit in, stand out and live the life you were created for.

Bibliography

Harland, Mike and Moser, Stan. *Seven Words of worship: the key to a lifetime of experiencing God.* Nashville. Tennessee: B&H Publishing Group, 2008.

Loho-u-Ter, Shadrach. *Tripartite Battlegrounds.* Gboko: Freelife press and publishers, 2014.

Warren, Rick. *Purpose Driven Life.* Grand Rapids: Zondervan, 2002.

Tracy, Brian. *The 100 absolutely unbreakable laws of business success.* San Francisco: Berrett-Koehler Publishers, inc, 2002.

Internet Resources

Gotquestions, "What is Christian ministry?" No Pages. Cited 30 July 2015. Online:

https://www.gotquestions.org/what-is-ministry.html.

Healthline, "Achieving a Balanced Diet." No Pages. Cited 27 July 2015. Online: https://www.healthline.com/health/balanced-diet#AchievingaBalancedDiet4.

King, Dan. "5 Ways You Can Care for the Environment." No Pages. Cited 30 July 2015. Online: https://www.patheos.com/blogs/thehighcalling/2015/04/global-care-activist-faith/.

Krejcir, Richard J. "How to Be a Christian in the Workplace." No Pages. Cited 30 July 2015. Online: www.discipleshiptools.org/apps/articles/default.asp?articleid=41215.

Psychology Today, "Living life purpose." No Pages. Cited 27 July 2015. Online: https://www.psychologytoday.com/blog/living-life-purpose.

Reachout, "What makes a good friend." No Pages. Cited 30 July 2015. Online:

https://www.au.reachout.com/what-makes-a-good-friend.

Reference Dictionary, "Enemy." No Pages. Cited 30 July 2015. Online: https://www.dictionary.reference.com/browse/enemy.

Santhosh, "Biblical Friendship - Who is a Friend?" No Pages. Cited 30 July 2015. Online: http://ccatenn.org/New_Creation/Articles/friend.asp.

Sharefaith, "What a friend we have in Jesus the song and the story." No Pages. Cited 30 July 2015. Online: visit http://www.sharefaith.com/guide/Christian-Music/hymns-the-songs-and-the-stories/what-a-friend-we-have-in-jesus-the-song-and-the-story.html.

Silvoso, Ed. "Anointed for Business." No Pages. Cited 30 July 2015. Online: http://www.intheworkplace.com/apps/articles/default.asp?articleid=12851&columnid=1935.

Sonnenberg, Frank. "7 ways to live life with a purpose." No Pages. Cited 27 July 2015. Online: https://www.franksonnenbergonline.com/blog/7-ways-to-live-life-with-a-purpose/.

Warren, Rick. "What on earth am I here for?" No Pages. Cited 30 July 2015. Online: https://pastors.com/what-on-earth-am-i-here-for/.

Other Books from Scrollhouse

Book for a Seminar

Scrollhouse Publishing Firm (A service of TheTheShepherd Loho-u-Ter Resources) conducts the following seminars and workshops:

-Authoring Masterclass
-Junior Authoring Masterclass
-Life Coaching workshop
-Editing workshop
-Leadership Workshops
-Admin Seminar
-Success Workshops
-Marriage Seminars

Contact us and book for a seminar in your organization.

scrollhouseng@gmail.com
www.scrollhouse.com.ng
+234-805-346-8634
+234-803-208-8168

www.ingramcontent.com/pod-product-compliance
Lightning Source LLC
Chambersburg PA
CBHW070524160726
48003CB00004B/1688